HERE, **TAKE THE WHEEL.**

SUCCESSION PLANNING STORIES AND INSIGHTS
FROM BUSINESS OWNERS

ISBN 978-0-615-25802-7

PUBLISHED BY PALMER PRINTING
739 SOUTH CLARK STREET
CHICAGO, IL 60605

TYPESET, PRINTED AND BOUND
IN THE UNITED STATES.

HERE, TAKE THE WHEEL.

SUCCESSION PLANNING STORIES AND INSIGHTS
FROM BUSINESS OWNERS

BY SARAH KRUGER, JAMES J. RAAF AND RICHARD P. SHUMA
INTRODUCTION BY ELLEN COSTELLO

CONTENTS

INTRODUCTION 6
ELLEN COSTELLO, CEO HARRIS BANKCORP, INC.

RIDING OUT THE STORM 10
BARBARA MOORE

END OF THE LINE 26
BRUCE RIDDELL

MOVER AND SHAKER 34
BRAD KOWALSKI

CHALLENGING TRADITION 42
LILY CHEN

ONE BIG HAPPY FAMILY...54
CHUCK LAWSON

FIRST YOU BUILD, THEN YOU SELL 64
MURRAY PRENTICE

KEEPING ON TRACK 72
THOMAS CARLISLE

A BICYCLE BUILT FOR TWO...82
TONY SABATINE

FROM THE OUTSIDE LOOKING IN...............................94
BRIAN TANNER

FINAL THOUGHTS ON SUCCESSION PLANNING.......102

INTRODUCTION

Successful entrepreneurs often spend a lifetime meticulously building the family business. Whether they begin by laying the foundation or building upon one already established by previous generations, the most successful business owners know that careful planning is often the key to thriving. So they plan for growth, they plan for change and they adjust their plan during challenging economic cycles.

Yet one plan that often is not considered can become the Achilles' heel of the family business – the plan for transfer of control, also known as succession planning. Ultimately, every owner of a closely held business must plan for the day when the enterprise that has been the center of his or her professional and economic life is transitioned to the next generation or sold entirely.

Why is succession planning so important? The most obvious answer is personal. A solid succession plan ensures that the enterprise continues to thrive as a source of economic security for the family. Then there is the idea of social responsibility, which is so often close to the heart of many business owners. The fact is that small business is increasingly important to the American economy. According to the U.S. Census Bureau, 65 percent of all U.S. businesses employ fewer than 100 individuals, and nearly 32 percent (63 million) of this country's paid employees work for these businesses.

Yet, as various studies show, the sad fact remains that only one in three family businesses will survive the transition to the second generation, and only one in ten will survive the transition to the third. Studies show, furthermore, that many of these businesses do not survive due to a lack of succession planning.

Why is succession planning so often overlooked by business owners? As we work with our clients at Harris, we find that there is no single reason. We know that typically business owners are "hands-on" managers. They tend to do everything themselves and are used to making all of the important decisions. Of course, just like everyone else, business owners want to enjoy all of the opportunities that life outside of the business offers. But the idea of allowing someone else to take the wheel of something as important and deeply personal as the family business can be difficult to accept.

Another reason behind the apparent reluctance of business owners to prepare for their retirement is the lack of a frame of reference. After all, independent business owners know how to run their business, but often have nothing to guide them on how to hand it over to someone new – even to a trusted son or daughter. Owners may feel they are entering unfamiliar territory while risking what is likely their most important asset.

Whatever the reason, lack of attention to the transition plan can result in a significant opportunity cost. Without a well-crafted succession plan, a business can easily fail in the transition to the next generation. Alternatively, if selling the business is the desired outcome, the lack of appropriate planning can have a negative impact on its ultimate value.

At Harris, we have given a great deal of thought to how we can help our clients deal with succession. We recognize that succession planning is part of a larger wealth management picture, and that a wide range of elements such as estate and trust planning, investment management and plans for philanthropy need to be considered.

The Harris organization has enjoyed many years of banking relationships with private businesses large and small. During that time, we have seen many businesses grow from early stage start-ups to successful, enduring corporations. We, as financial and business partners, feel responsible for the long-term success of our clients, just as they feel responsible for the well-being of their employees.

With that in mind, we offer *Here, Take the Wheel. Succession Planning Stories and Insights from Business Owners*, a collection of some of our clients' succession planning experiences (both good and bad) with businesses just like your own. Each family profiled in this book has started to address their own succession planning issues and decisions. Their experiences are real; however, the names and nature of the businesses involved have been changed to respect the privacy of the families. By sharing their stories, we hope to help other families realize that business owners share common concerns. Our goal is to help business owners identify workable solutions to these issues and make financially sound decisions.

Throughout our history, Harris has helped thousands of business owners – our clients – navigate the sometimes choppy waters of succession planning. By building a plan, just as they have built a plan for the operation of their business, business owners dramatically enhance the chance of reaching their goals. This is not to say that the first plan developed is the one that is ultimately implemented. As is the case when addressing most business issues, flexibility is crucial, and commitment to the process, rather than the event, is the key to success.

The stories of individual owners contained in this book capture a wide range of perspectives on dealing with the complexities of succession planning. In the course of my travels across the country, I have been fortunate enough to meet with many owners of family businesses. As they talk about their own plans for succession, it becomes clear that each situation is unique and there can be no cookie-cutter approach to dealing with the complex business, family and emotional issues that are often intertwined. Yet, as these stories illustrate, there are many valuable lessons to be learned, both from the experiences of other families and from the expertise of specialized advisors.

It is my hope that the paths chosen by these families may serve as a point of reference for you and your family and that they will inspire, and perhaps advance, your own thinking around the critical issue of succession planning.

Ellen Costello,
Chief Executive Officer
Harris Bankcorp, Inc.

1

RIDING OUT THE STORM

Barbara Moore learned many lessons through the unexpected obstacles she faced in running the family business. By sharing her perspective, Barbara hopes to help other families deal with the challenges of succession.

Barbara Moore is an energetic, entrepreneurial woman who has successfully coped with personal- and business-related challenges. Her husband, Frank, was an engineer who founded a company making customized packaging equipment. Following their marriage, Barbara worked full time in the business and helped it grow to a point where it was averaging annual sales in excess of $80 million.

Frank's sudden death was not only a crushing personal loss for Barbara, it also came at a time when the very future of the business was threatened. The company was experiencing its worst corporate year ever, working capital was in very short supply and there were no life insurance funds available to ease the situation.

As a result of good fortune, hard work and composure in the face of major challenges, Barbara successfully kept the business afloat and, in recent years, has achieved even greater growth by expanding into new markets. Her only child, Dan, has worked in the business since graduation and will carry it forward into the next generation. Dan's forthcoming marriage has raised several estate planning issues, which Barbara has taken steps to address.

When my husband started the business 40 years ago, he was the only employee. Now we have close to 300 people on the payroll, so we have come a long way. After college, I had a position in the advertising department of our local newspaper. I met Frank through a mutual friend and in 1970, he persuaded me to come and work for him, which I have never regretted. Frank was 20 years older than me, but we made a great team and eventually we got married. Frank was the engineer, and I was basically everything else from representing the company as the chief financial officer to taking care of human resources, marketing and client relationships. My husband was never much of a money guy so I also handled anything that had to do with borrowing and lending, as well!

Over the decades, we grew the business together. If it was an engineering problem, it went to Frank; if it was a finance problem, it came to me. That's how we divided the business. Together, we experienced pretty much everything you can experience in a business. And like everyone else, we thought that nothing unexpected would ever happen, but it did.

Despite their usual harmonious working relationship, there were a few issues on which the couple disagreed. One of them was the need for life insurance.

Frank's position was that he wanted to put money back into the company, not put it into life insurance. He felt there was no need to pay those huge premiums on life insurance when we could handle the situation ourselves. "You will be fine if anything happens to me, and I will be fine if anything happens to you," he always said.

I couldn't convince him otherwise, but I certainly had reason to do so following the death of my sister. I've always had a number of other entrepreneurial interests besides my involvement with the business. One of them was a fabric store that came up for sale in our community. I thought it might be fun to buy it if I could get my sister to come and manage it for me. She was widowed and was very happy to move closer to us and have something to occupy her time. She ran the store successfully for several years but, just as we were expanding into a new location, she was diagnosed with pancreatic cancer and died shortly thereafter.

I did not have any kind of back-up plan or anyone to assume her management role. Also, I did not have life insurance coverage in her name. When she died it was a personal loss, of course, but I was also very much affected by her absence at the store and found I needed to put in working capital to keep things afloat.

At this point, I pinned Frank down and insisted that we address our own insurance situation. We eventually compromised on split dollar life insurance which brought the cost down to a point that Frank could accept. Under the terms of the policy, none of the $10 million pay-out would come due until the death of the second person so, in essence, when Frank died the life insurance would become active but it wouldn't pay anything until my passing. At that point, the proceeds would go into a trust with our son named as the ultimate beneficiary.

It was 1992 when we finally got the insurance in place, so for more than 20 years we had operated without any kind of coverage or planning. Like many people in business, we were very naive and never thought about how things could change in a snap.

As events unfolded, it was fortuitous that the Moores had taken out life insurance when they did.

Not long after the insurance was in place, Frank developed some serious health problems — first, a brush with cancer and then a cardiac condition that required open-heart surgery. Both of these issues came as a total surprise since Frank was always the picture of health and prided himself on his level of fitness. At the time his cancer was diagnosed, it suddenly dawned on me that he was now uninsurable for any sizable amount.

Of course, the biggest shock came when Frank died very unexpectedly in 2003. It was a Saturday and all three of us — Frank, Dan and I — were at the plant going over some financials. At the end of our discussion, Frank said he was going to change and go for a jog around the grounds. He came back in terrible shape, said his chest hurt and that he needed to sit down. Then he slumped over and that was it. He was 71 years old at the time.

The loss of her husband was not the only challenge that Barbara faced that year.

Prior to Frank's death, the business was going through a really tough time and sales were in a slump. We knew we had some good prospects but the orders were just not coming in. When Frank passed away so unexpectedly, you could sense the employees were worried about their own situations. It was only natural for them to be concerned about what was going to happen.

Establishing a calm and stable atmosphere at the plant became a priority for Barbara despite her personal sense of loss and grief.

Even before Frank's death, I knew it was not going to be a good year from a sales point of view. After his passing, there was an even greater need to establish a sense of calmness and stability. On the day of the visitation, I was at the plant and right after the funeral, I was at the plant. Dan and I never missed a beat;

I was always there. Even now, after all the years I have spent in the business, I am never away for more than a few days at a time. I feel that maintaining a routine sends an important message to the employees.

Despite the fact that the sales outlook was not great, I chose not to lay people off or adjust working hours. I just tried to hold steady and make sure that everything was as normal as possible.

While Barbara was doing her best to maintain the status quo, she was forced to deal with cash flow problems resulting from a lack of sales.

As a result of sales being down, we were experiencing cash flow problems. I knew I would have to put money into the business to get us through to the point where the orders would hopefully start coming in. We did have two insurance policies that paid out a total of $1.5 million, but none of the $10 million life insurance we had put in place was payable at that time. The arrangement we had set up didn't help at a time when we probably needed it the most.

To make matters worse, the bankers we had at the time were less than helpful. Essentially they said, "We know you are tight on working capital right now, but you have enough personal resources so you don't need us." I was forced to put close to $4 million of my own money back into the business. So when it came right down to it, I went through the worst time in my business and personal life with a lender who wouldn't help me through it.

Barbara's determination to stay the course eventually paid off with a sudden influx of orders.

The year of my husband's death was our worst corporate year ever. I felt everyone was just watching and waiting to see what would happen. Then in December, we took in $30 million worth of orders. Essentially, all of the orders that were pending came through. While that was very good news, it also resulted in a new challenge for the business. Since our sales had been down, we were sitting with a depleted inventory and, suddenly, we had to go into high production. The cost of going from low-to-high production is very significant, but we were lucky in that we had kept our workforce in place, and we were able to meet the orders as they came in. As a matter of fact, 2003 was our worst year ever but 2004 turned out to be our third-best year ever. It was an amazing turn around.

Barbara feels she learned a number of valuable lessons from the experience.

It confirmed for me the value of being steadfast and trying to keep conditions stable. Nothing good ever comes from acting panicked.

Although we were able to get through the situation without the life insurance we had arranged, it would have been much better if I could have used the proceeds of a policy instead of putting in my own money.

The upheaval of 2003 made me realize it was time to look for a new bank that would be more receptive to our needs. Our new bank has an appreciation of the kind of business we operate. The kind of packaging equipment we produce is highly customized and the machines are paid for by progress payments as they move through production. For example, an initial deposit of 25 percent is required and then supplementary payments are made as the order moves through production, to delivery, to performance.

Our new bank considers the progress payments as contingent liabilities, whereas the previous relationship was with a cash flow type of lender that didn't want to know you during the hard times. A good bank understands that sooner or later a bad year will occur, whether as the result of a downturn in the economy, the death of an owner, a change in product lines or a need to diversify. A lending institution that is prepared to hold firm with you during those challenging times and truly understands your company is the best partner a business can ever have.

Apart from dealing with financial issues, Barbara had many other business-related challenges during the period following Frank's death.

When Frank passed away, he was not replaced. I simply took over his workload. My approach was that everything was going to continue as before. His death happened so quickly that most people didn't have the time to worry about it or mull over the repercussions. Frank was gone, but the business was still there and Dan and I were there.

However, some of our employees started asking questions. In particular, they wanted to know if the business was going to be sold. Sometimes, they had questions that were very insensitive and hurtful, but I still had to respect them for asking. After all, they needed to know what was going on and how it would affect their lives.

My answer was always, "No, we are not going to sell the business. Dan is going to be in charge one day and, until then, I am going to take my turn at it. We are a good company, and we are moving forward and looking to become even more successful."

It was very important to provide reassurance to everyone,

because a business is its employees and the last thing you need following the death of an owner is to see your people heading out the door. I made a point of sticking closely to the business – I still do – and I think my constant presence in the office sent the right message of consistency and stability.

Fortunately for Barbara, she could rely on the assistance and support of her son, Dan, in the aftermath of the sudden loss of her husband.

Thankfully, Dan was right there in place and couldn't have shown more devotion. He works 60 to 80 hours per week, and I couldn't ask for a more disciplined partner. If anything, I think he wants to grow the business too quickly and this is a bit of an issue between us. For the most part, we are able to work through our differences; although, at this point, I do have the final say. Nonetheless, I always consult him and involve him in the process.

Dan's involvement in the business has always been "a given" in the Moore family.

We always assumed that Dan would enter the business. Ever since he understood what we did and where our money came from, he was preparing to be in the business. From a very young age, he showed a lot of entrepreneurial ability. When he was only seven years old we bought him a tractor to mow lawns as a first communion gift. He set up a business mowing lawns for money and became totally self-sufficient! Unlike most kids, he never asked for, or received, an allowance. During high school, he was involved with other money-making propositions. He understood that his parents had an ongoing business, that we both worked at it for the betterment of the family, and that he was part of it. He always worked summers at the plant, and it was just assumed

that, after college, he would come into the business and make
machines because that is what the Moore family does.

Dan graduated with an engineering degree, but he is excellent at
handling money matters as well. He loves the challenge of selling
our products and works hard at establishing good relations with
our customers. He is very much like his father in that regard.

At some point, I am sure that Dan will go back to school and get
an MBA. A number of years ago, before Frank passed away, Dan
applied to get into an Executive MBA program. It was something
both Frank and I thought he needed, and we felt it would be
very beneficial to the future of the company. However, he wasn't
accepted, because they said he did not have sufficient workplace
experience. At this point in his career, he has plenty of experi-
ence, but it's much harder for him to step away from the business
to go back to school. Even though it would involve a big sacrifice
for him to do so, I would be very supportive if he chose to do it.

Apart from being Barbara's right-hand man, Dan is also Barbara's
sole heir. As a result of the lessons learned from previous experience, Barbara has spent a considerable amount of time consulting
with experts on the orderly transition of family assets.

At the time of Frank's death, he owned all the shares in the
business. This was as a result of a prenuptial agreement that we
never bothered to change even after I became an equal participant
in the business. When Frank died, I inherited all those shares.
During our marriage, I acquired many other assets – real estate,
a couple of small businesses and a significant investment portfo-
lio – all of which I held in my own name. So, with Frank's death,
I became a one-woman show. With the exception of a family trust
that was set up with a generational skip, I now own everything.
Since Dan is my only child, he is the logical beneficiary. I have no
concerns about his ability to handle this wealth since, at 30 years

of age, he is a responsible, well-educated businessman.

A complicating factor in this situation is that Dan has a fiancée and plans to be married later this year.

Ever since Dan advised me of his intentions, I have known that I could not will to him in the way I had originally planned because of the issue of common property. For example, the $10 million in life insurance payable on my death could be considered marital property. There is some protection that could be achieved through a prenuptial agreement, but the two people involved can change a prenuptial at any time.

By working closely with our attorney, I have come up with an arrangement that will avoid putting Dan in a position of exposure. The plan we have established calls for all of my assets (with the exception of the family trust) to go into a trust at the time of my death. Dan will be a trustee, along with two other trustees, and they will jointly determine a distribution that is appropriate for Dan. The $10 million life insurance payment is a particular concern of mine, and we are now in the process of transferring that into a new and separate trust so that the proceeds can never be considered common property.

Our attorney has been outstanding in protecting the business in case my son is ever involved in a divorce settlement. The trust in which my assets will be held is strong in that it regulates Dan, but it also gives Dan the power to regulate his spouse in the event things fall apart. The family trust money has regulations and boundaries controlling the uses to which the money can be put. In addition, before my trust pays out anything to Dan, he has to reaffirm with his wife that the prenuptial has not been changed or eliminated. If it has, then his employment in the business will be jeopardized and his access to my estate will be curtailed.

Barbara has taken such decisive action because she feels that divorce or re-marriage pose some of the biggest risk exposures that family-owned businesses face.

I think Dan truly understands why I am going to these great lengths to protect our business, our assets and our family wealth. Certainly, I hope that Dan will stay happily married and there won't be a divorce, but obviously you can never tell what the future may bring. Theirs is a very one-sided prenuptial. Dan will eventually have great wealth, but Stephanie essentially brings nothing to the table other than love and companionship. When a marriage breaks down, the love and companionship disappear but the money stays on the table. That is why you have to protect your assets and why I am helping Dan protect them. The plans that I have made also address the possibility of a second marriage by putting the same procedures in place. This ensures that future generations will always be protected.

I think Frank and I did a good job of communicating with Dan our desire for the business to remain in the family. So far he has done everything we could ask of him. Eventually, I hope he will pass on that sense of family commitment to his children; in the meantime, all I can do is protect the wealth, and pass it on, and then it will be up to him.

Barbara currently has not fixed a date on which she plans to retire, preferring to leave her options open.

There's no denying we're all getting older, and Dan asks me every once in a while when I am going to retire. My answer to that question is that I have no firm plans. I believe I will just know when I no longer feel like I'm on top of my game for what-ever reason – feeling tired, or sick, or simply having a change in attitude. I'll be the first to know and I will exit at a time when

*it will not hurt the business and I am comfortable that we have
good people in place.*

*In the meantime, I have a few goals left to accomplish, includ-
ing the establishment of an advisory board. I used to criticize
Frank for not having a board of directors and, after his passing,
I considered establishing one. It didn't take me long, however,
to realize that I preferred to hire professionals in an advisory
capacity since their sole objective was to benefit me and help
the business meet its objectives. However, a number of years
have gone by since Frank's passing and I can see the value of
forming an advisory board to help establish new goals and
objectives, especially in the area of future expansion through
product diversification.*

At this point in her life, Barbara can afford to be somewhat
philosophical as she ponders what the future may bring for
her son and reflects on lessons learned following the loss of
her husband.

*If a business isn't doing well prior to the death of an owner,
chances are it is not going to survive the loss. However, if the
business is successful, there are steps that can be taken to ensure
its continued growth and success in spite of the planned or, in
our case, unplanned exit of the owner. The following are some
of the lessons I have learned:*

1) PUT GROWTH IN PERSPECTIVE
*It isn't necessary to have growth every year. During times of
trauma or tight economic conditions, it is better to reduce debt
and let the business become stronger. Growth is costly and, at a
time when more unknowns have come into a business, it is best
to simply maintain consistency and stability.*

2) ENSURE LIFE INSURANCE IS IMMEDIATELY AVAILABLE

Based on my own situation, I cannot stress this enough. Life insurance is simply essential for the continuing life and management of the business. The amount should be equal to the debt the business carries and additional term insurance should be purchased as well. If there is sufficient life insurance in place, the business does not have to liquidate any assets and personal wealth does not get mixed in with the corporate cash flow and capitalization. Also, life insurance provides the funds to at least initiate the process of buying out a spouse or a child if that is what they wish.

I believe that trusts should be in place for the protection of the life insurance so that the funds get channeled into the business rather than into the hands of an individual. Individuals can get caught up in their own personal situations and, at the time of a business owner's death, money is a key issue. Having good trust and business attorneys should be an integral part of the succession planning process. They can advise on matters such as the need to move additional money into the trust to support the growth of the business.

3) STAY THE COURSE

It is essential to hold the business steady, no matter what. In my case, I had to use my own personal wealth. I'm only grateful I had the means and I never hesitated for a moment. If a business owner's family is not committed to the business, I think there can be real problems in store. A family business, by definition, involves more than one family member and they all have to be committed.

4) CONTAIN COSTS

When a business is exposed to changes in ownership or new management, it is not the time to make any major, rash decisions.

It is best to defer any action that will lead to an increase in costs until the business is on a firmer footing.

5) RETAIN KEY EMPLOYEES

A successful business is one that is able to retain its key employees. Good managers are hard to find and, once you invest 4–6 years in them, they become instrumental. During a period of change or trauma, it's essential to keep those employees who have been with you for years, who know the business inside and out, and who can provide the consistency that is so important.

6) GET GOOD LEGAL REPRESENTATION

The reality of being a business owner is that you will require a great deal of legal counsel on everything from paying the proper taxes and developing hiring procedures, to establishing holding structures and entering into contracts. Every business needs to allocate sufficient funds for good legal representation and this fact cannot be overemphasized.

7) BUILD A GOOD RELATIONSHIP WITH YOUR BANK

Having a good relationship with a bank or lending institution is invaluable for every business owner in the day-to-day operations of his or her business. At a time of change or trauma, this relationship becomes even more critically important. I value our relationship with our bank and our legal representatives more highly than anything else. For me, they represent my security blankets.

8) EDUCATE SPOUSES

At the time of the death of an owner, there are a tremendous number of personal and emotional issues to deal with. If the surviving spouse does not have at least a basic understanding of the family-owned business, the situation is compounded by all of the financial- and business-related factors that must be addressed.

This can result in a nightmare situation where good people leave and the business is thrown into disarray. Owners should ensure their spouses are educated to at least a point from which they can make informed decisions, should the need arise.

9) BE AWARE OF WEAKNESSES

However smooth the operation appears, or how much profit is brought in, every business has areas of weakness. I believe that most business owners concentrate on what makes them money and, if something concerns them, they tend to push it to the side as long as the business is making a profit. Perhaps an owner knows that he requires product diversification or that one business area will require capital expenditures. These are the kinds of things I would classify as weaknesses. These concerns are the last thing a business needs to address on the unexpected departure of an owner. Working on these areas of weakness and getting the business strong on a day-to-day basis should be a priority.

In my own situation, I have an independent audit conducted every year. The auditors just come in and look at the books—they don't care who I am or what we do. Essentially, they give me a report card on the business. Using their objective insight, they might advise me that our warranty is too high or our inventory is too low. Independent auditors can tell an owner where the weaknesses are. They're an outside source that calls it straight. Without this kind of monitoring, businesses can be tainted in a number of ways and ownership can become complacent or confused about where the business is going.

10) PUT YOUR BUSINESS FIRST

Regardless of who you are, what you do or what kind of person you are, if you own a business, then the business comes first. You have a commitment not only to yourself and to your family, but also to your employees. It is your employees who create the success you enjoy, and no business of any size is a one-person show.

I have employees who sometimes drive me crazy, but when I look at them and see them welding those machines and pushing the product out of the door, I know I should put my personal feelings aside. Employees, managers and owners – we all need to put the business first. Whether good, bad or indifferent, it provides a life for all of us, and the more we pull together, the better it is for everyone.

11) SEE CHANGE AS AN OPPORTUNITY

Owning a business is a great opportunity, but it involves a lot of risk-taking and that's something you just have to get your head around. One of the key qualities of a good businessperson is the ability he or she has to address change. I believe in taking a chance and assuming some risk. If someone gives me a negative response, I will typically say, "I don't want to hear why you can't do it, just scramble and give me the result." My employees will tell you that "scramble" is one of my favorite words! To me, it sums up the process of being flexible, adapting to change and thinking under duress. One of the weaknesses of our company is that we have only had three layoffs in over 40 years, so we need to guard against complacency in the workplace. I have to make sure that, when people come to work, they know they're required to "scramble" for the business.

2
END OF THE LINE

Bruce Riddell is the second-generation owner of a major producer of heavy building materials. Based in Arizona, Bruce also oversees operations in Florida and California. A wide range of products is manufactured including cement, crushed stone, concrete pipe and asphalt.

The business came about as a result of a merger in 1987. Bruce and his father own 35 percent of the operation while two other partners have an equal interest in the balance of the equity.

Since Bruce does not want to have children, his succession planning is focused on the eventual sale of the business.

I came on the scene in 1997 – ten years after the merger took place. Prior to that, I had spent five years working in public accounting doing tax planning for high-net-worth individuals and business owners.

When my dad offered me the chance to get involved and receive an equity stake in the company, it was too good of an opportunity to turn down. I was very aware, though, that the perception might be that my father was handing out a job to a family member. Fortunately, I had the advantage of having some pretty solid credentials when I walked in the door. The fact is, as the boss's son, you're always going to be looked at differently. Right from the start, I think that as long as everything went okay, the employees knew I would be the one taking over the business.

Since joining the company, Bruce's role has evolved and he is now assuming a far greater responsibility in the overall management.

I came in as controller and, as I gained more experience in handling the finances of the business, I progressed into the position of chief financial officer. As my father gets closer to retirement, I am working more in the capacity of chief operating officer.

My father and I make all of the day-to-day decisions. I work very well with him. We tend to think identically and it's actually a lot of fun running the business with him. From a practical standpoint, it's also great to have two sets of eyes overseeing everything.

Our other two partners are retired, but the four of us continue to meet somewhat informally once a month to discuss various issues. We do have an annual shareholders' meeting, which is a more formal affair. Essentially, the partners serve as a kind of advisory team. We are all rational beings—we talk about things, we talk through things and we are successful.

Bruce enjoys an excellent relationship with the other principals in the business.

When you first start working with people, it naturally takes time to gain their trust before they turn the reins over to you. We have been very lucky in that the business has effectively doubled in size in the 10 years since I came on board. When you are successful and things are constantly improving, there is a lot more to be excited about and to work towards achieving. We concentrate on the positive things and spend very little time arguing about things that don't matter.

Although we have seldom, if ever, had any significant disagreements, we do have a mechanism for majority rule by voting interest. The voting shares are split equally three ways between my dad and the other two partners. Disputes can be settled by a two-to-one vote, although a unanimous vote would be required to sell the business. At this time, I have a non-voting share, but that is merely to avoid complicating the situation and will obviously change over time.

Bruce firmly believes in the maxim that the people running the business should be the owners of the business.

From time to time, we've discussed the issue of inactive children of partners having voting shares. Basically, we've always come to the conclusion that – if they're not involved in the business – then they can bring very little value to the decision-making process. Speaking personally, I would strongly oppose having inactive shareholders, such as my partners' children, telling me how to run the business or making decisions on compensation. If we were ever to go the route of having inactive family members own shares, then it would be in a non-voting capacity. From my own perspective, though, I still think it's best to keep family members out of the ownership role. There are plenty of other ways to provide compensation.

Bruce's business has many of the qualities of a family-run operation, but he does not foresee family ownership extending beyond his generation.

We consider ourselves a closely held family business. We aren't a family business in the traditional sense of one family owning the entire business, but we definitely operate like a family business.

*One of our partners has a son who has a job in our sales depart-
ment, but he is the only other family member currently involved
in the business. He does not have any ownership position and, to
my knowledge, is not looking to move beyond his position in the
sales department.*

*For my own part, I do not plan to have any children so, eventu-
ally, someone will be taking over the business as the result of a
sale. Exactly what form that sale will take isn't clear to me yet
but, in my mind, the end game is a sale.*

Soon after the merger that created the company, an agreement
was reached that addressed the eventuality of one of the partners
passing away or choosing to sell his share.

*The original buy/sell agreement has been updated many times,
but the principle remains the same: the remaining shareholders
will buy out the shares. We have not provided for a shareholder
to pass on his shares to a family member or heir.*

*Eventually, I expect the business to fall to me since I will have
to buy out the shares of the partners on their passing. They will
hold their interests as long as they are alive, they want to remain
shareholders and we are happy to have them as partners. When
the inevitable occurs, we have life insurance in place to help with
the buyout.*

Communicating the owners' intentions to the company's management team has been an integral part of the succession plan.

*We have a number of long-term employees who have made a
significant contribution to the building of this company. I think
we owe it to them to be clear at all times regarding our succession
plan. If you have multiple people competing for similar positions,*

you are going to run into issues. The sooner you clear up any uncertainties, the better. That may be an oversimplification, but I do believe that the simple process of communication early on in the game goes a long way to avoiding disputes.

All of the partners participated in the succession planning process and were able to reach agreement through consensus.

We have a track record of being able to come to terms amicably and the bottom line is that we were able to agree among ourselves what would be fair to each owner and what would be fair to the heirs. For those reasons, we did not hire a succession consultant but I'm sure that many other businesses would benefit from assistance in working through the process.

The most difficult conversations we had were with respect to valuing the company for the purposes of the buy/sell. This was something we struggled with over a period of time. Obviously, a seller is going to want a different valuation than the person who is going to take on that liability.

Bruce's accounting background has enabled him to address the issue of valuation in a calculated manner.

We looked at a variety of multiples of Earnings before Interest, Tax and Amortization (EBITA). Essentially, the valuation process comes down to what multiple you place on the company. There are a range of options to choose from. Our partners have ties to venture capitalists and learned from them approximately which multiple should be used. I had my own opinions, and we met somewhere in the middle around the 4 to 6 range.

Bruce is hopeful that the current ownership structure will continue as long as possible.

When you start a company, there is often very little capital involved, but when you grow it over a number of years, you end up with a lot of money tied up in the business. For this reason, we don't want to buy out our partners at this time. Both my father and I are basically conservative, and the last thing we want is to take on a huge amount of debt at a time when we are finally in a position of having very little debt. For my dad, it would be like starting over if he had to take on millions of dollars of debt to buy out the other shareholders. In addition, the price issue would undoubtedly come up again.

Accordingly, we are committed to continuing our relationship with our partners. They know the business, and they are not placing unreasonable expectations on us. It's a great investment for them, too. Where else could they get an annualized return of 20 percent to 30 percent on their investment?

WHAT THE ADVISORS SAY

In Bruce's case, the succession plan is quite evident – he wishes to sell the business as he has no plans to have children. Fortunately for Bruce, he is able to direct his attention to practical matters rather than getting caught up in the "soft issues" that can monopolize succession planning when there are family members involved.

Since a sale of the business is the desired goal, Bruce should concentrate his efforts on improving operating efficiencies and strengthening the management team to make the business more appealing to potential buyers.

NEXT STEPS

BUSINESS VALUATIONS

Since Bruce will need to buy out the shares of his partners when they exit, it is important to reach agreement on a standard method of valuing the company's shares. In addition, when setting the value of the company for a sale, a somewhat different calculation may be used and that calculation should be clearly established. Bruce would be well advised to hire outside experts for the purpose of establishing the business's valuation and conducting an annual review thereafter.

PREPARING FOR A SALE

The business should be managed strategically to appeal to the widest universe of potential buyers. Future decisions such as entering new markets and territories, or making additions to the product line, should all be considered not only on their economic merits but also in terms of the impact they will have on improving the attractiveness of the business to potential buyers.

A substantial portion of the universe of buyers is made up of private equity firms. Not only do these firms look for sound business characteristics, but for sound management teams as well. The company might be wise to implement a long-term compensation plan for their key managers in order to retain them as a valuable part of the business for the private equity firm. Few businesses maximize sale value without such a plan in place.

Establishing a long-term incentive plan may be another attractive means of supporting and enhancing management and building loyalty.

ESTATE MAXIMIZATION

While the business owners have taken a "go-at-it-alone" approach, they would find it advantageous to hire a professional financial planner to help with minimizing taxation for the exiting partners and executing an appropriate format to cash out their shares.

3

MOVER AND SHAKER

Ever since childhood, Brad Kowalski has been fascinated by heavy equipment. Having moved on from the toy bulldozers of his sandbox days, he now is the proud owner of one of the largest construction equipment dealerships in the Midwest. Starting out as a mechanic in his teens, Brad's continuing interest has been in developing the service aspect of the business he now owns. He has already established a number of satellite service locations and is looking to expand in this area. The demand is certainly there from customers who appreciate the reduction in downtime afforded by a quick turn around.

Having worked so hard to establish his business, Brad is determined to keep it in the family. All four of his children are actively engaged in the business, and he looks forward to seeing them carry on the tradition into the next generation.

All through high school, I helped out at a local auto repair shop. Fixing stuff just seemed to come naturally to me, and I can't say I ever had any doubts about what I'd end up doing. Never in my wildest dreams, though, did I imagine I'd achieve the kind of success I have.

As soon as I got out of trade school, I got a job at a nearby heavy equipment dealership — working on toys for "big boys." The owner and I got on great. He liked my work, and pretty soon I was the service manager. Over the years, as his health declined, he began to show me different parts of the operation and I learned a lot from him. He gave me a share of the business, and when he passed away the bank put together a plan to help me buy the rest. It sounds kind of hokey, but I guess I was the son he never had.

The nature of the heavy equipment service trade has changed dramatically from the 1970s when Brad got his start.

Back then, you'd often have to just tear things apart to find out the problem. Nowadays, there are all kinds of fancy diagnostics. I like to say we went from the Stone Age to the Space Age, and it seemed to happen almost overnight.

Suddenly, you weren't looking for general mechanics but specialized technicians able to work on very large, expensive equipment. New equipment sales are dependent on our service reputation, and minimizing downtime is critical. By the mid-1980s, we had a real shortage of techs on our hands and that situation continues to this day. Part of the problem is that the birthrate keeps dropping and there are fewer kids coming out of high school, period. Also, a lot of people are turning their noses up at being in a trade. You probably don't have too many young people saying that after high school they want to be mechanics. If you don't get introduced to this trade by someone in the business, you are probably not going to get involved. And, despite all the computer diagnostics, the work is still hard, dirty and time consuming at the mechanic level.

Brad has been fortunate in that all four of his children have expressed an interest in entering the business.

As the business began to grow and expand, I naturally started thinking about succession planning. I went to a seminar on the topic, and the specialist there said the only solution for business owners in my industry was to have more kids! As far as he was concerned, the answer to the labor shortage and the succession issue was to get your family involved in the business. Now, I'm not saying that's the reason my wife and I had four children, but I did start bringing my kids into the business as early as I could.

I did not give my children any conditions, such as gaining outside experience, before they entered the business. I guess it's a good idea in theory but, in my business, there is such a labor shortage that I was happy just to have another body. As our business grows and diversifies in the future, I can see that the next generation might want to establish some guidelines in this regard.

With three sons and a daughter all actively involved in the business, Brad is able to benefit from their various skills and interests.

My eldest son is 27. When he was 15, he started working in the shop – cleaning up and learning the trade. Now he is our chief operating officer. I have to say that I never thought he would rise to that level – and certainly not at such a young age. He has really surprised me in a very pleasant way. I am extremely lucky because Tyler is such a likeable person. When you are 20 years old and you have to give instruction to people who are much older, it's only natural to expect some resistance on their part. Tyler somehow has the ability to ask people what they think should be done, rather than telling them what to do. The end result is that the job gets done and done well.

My daughter, who graduated from college, works in our marketing department and also is a big help to me in other aspects of the business. My middle son is a hands-on production guy; he went to trade school to prepare himself for this work. He would rather have the day-to-day involvement of servicing equipment and interacting with the customers. My youngest son is just getting involved at the entry level, so I'm not sure where his interests will lie.

Open communication with family members on a regular basis has become a tradition in the Kowalski family.

It was my wife's suggestion that we bring the whole gang to-gether once a month to keep everybody in the picture. So, on the third Sunday of each month, we have a family meeting with our children and their spouses and fiancées. The setting may be informal, but we have an agenda and go over all of the aspects of the business. I think it's important to bring everybody together so we are all on the same page and understand what the next steps will be. Apart from the dealership, I own real estate and a storage locker business, and I also have an interest in a waste manage-ment operation. Most of these are passive investments, but some require active involvement.

I lead these meetings and my sense is that they are going well and bringing the family closer together. We don't have a family mission statement at this time, but I think that it is a worthwhile objective, so we are going to work on developing one.

I believe that spouses should know what their partners are involved in. It helps them to understand the importance of family and to have an appreciation of our reputation in the community. In a service industry like ours, we should always aim to be courteous and to treat people well.

While Brad has given some initial consideration to the succession planning process, he will need to refine his plans as his children's roles become more established.

Over the next few years, my goal is to have each of my children established as a division head – all reporting to my oldest son – who has naturally risen to a leadership role. Other than a written will, I have not thought further about the details of my children being in the business. My will was written with the assumption that all of my children will be in an equal position and it divides everything equally.

At this point, everything is running smoothly, but I think it's because I'm still running the show. If I wasn't around, and they all had an equal interest, would they still have the same commitment and energy level as they do now? I don't think so and that could definitely be a problem. At this point, I have to take a wait and see attitude and give them time to fill their positions. But I do worry what would happen if something happened to me in the meantime. Initially, my wife would be in control, since when I die, it all goes to her. She has never been involved in the business so the kids would have to fend for themselves and work out some kind of an arrangement. The last thing I would want is for my family to get involved in some kind of struggle over finances. I want their focus to be on the business of serving our customers.

By his own reckoning, Brad is still more than 15 years from retirement and hopes this will be ample time to solidify the foundations of a lasting family enterprise.

My goal is to retire at age 69. That will give me an even 50 years in the business. I will just walk away and take a dividend – and let my kids continue to run the business. I think it will be a proud moment for me, and I look forward to watching my kids take the business to the next level.

While new equipment sales are an obvious need, service is the lifeblood of the company. The business I'm in is strictly a service business. You have to care about people and be passionate about what you do. For me, the money has always been secondary. I would never have gotten any real satisfaction from passive ownership. Looking to the future, I value the fact that my children are all actively involved in various aspects of the operation. I hope it stays that way for a very long time.

WHAT THE ADVISORS SAY

Brad is to be congratulated on parlaying a childhood interest in toy bulldozers into a thriving heavy construction equipment dealership. Given the difficulties he faces in attracting new employees, it is fortunate that all four of his children have expressed an interest in working for the family business. It appears that Brad's children are performing admirably in the business with no apparent sibling rivalry, at least while Brad is at the helm. Conducting regular family meetings may well be contributing to this positive atmosphere.

Despite Brad's confidence in the developing skills of his children, they are still relatively young. While Brad achieved success by going directly into the business, it may be helpful to get the kids involved in industry groups or other leadership training to broaden their exposure.

Brad has stated that his retirement is still 15 years away. In the meantime, the company faces a considerable degree of risk in the event of unforeseen circumstances. The biggest challenge facing Brad at this point in time is developing a contingency plan in the event of death, disability or other unforeseen circumstances.

NEXT STEPS

ESTATE PLANS

In referring to his current estate plan, Brad at one point states that the business will be split four ways, but then he also mentions that, upon his death, "everything goes to his wife." Apparent contradictions such as these need to be thought through and clarified. Brad says he doesn't want his children to be engaged in a "struggle over finances," but it is clearly not in the best interests of the business to expect them to fend for themselves and work out a deal. It would make sense for Brad to work with an estate specialist to ensure that his intentions are clear and his wishes are carried out.

In addition, Brad should seek professional advice regarding the liquidity needs that may arise from a potentially substantial estate tax.

OWNERSHIP SUCCESSION AND BUY/SELL AGREEMENTS

Brad would benefit from a framework for ownership succession in the next generation. He needs to spend some time building a family buy/sell arrangement as well as outlining a structure for redeeming family members' interest in the business should they no longer wish to stay with the business. This issue is the single greatest factor in families being driven apart after the death of the founder.

Business owners have a wide range of options to pursue to tailor an effective buy/sell agreement. The agreement will need to change over time, but it can be tailored to specific business and family situations.

RETIREMENT INCOME

Brad refers to "walking away and taking a dividend" when he retires. However, there are a number of structures that can provide retirement income to the founder that are more tax efficient. Brad would be well advised to seek professional assistance in addressing this and other estate planning issues in order to reduce the strain on the business and the family in the long run.

4

CHALLENGING TRADITION

At the age of 27, Lily Chen is a trailblazer in a culture that is traditionally male dominated. Lily is a first generation American – the only child of Taiwanese parents who settled in California's Bay Area in the late 1970s. During Lily's childhood, her father, Calvin, was frequently absent as he strove to grow his business of manufacturing and wholesaling high-end baby supplies and accessories. Lily spent much of her time with her traditional stay-at-home mother. She set her sights on a liberal arts education and had no desire to become involved in the ups and downs of the family business.

Around the time of Lily's graduation from college, all of the hard work put in by her father and his brothers paid off. The brand became an overnight success, and Calvin began to see the business as a valuable asset that could be the foundation of a lasting family legacy. In most traditional Asian families, it is the custom for the eldest son to take over the family business, but that was obviously not an option for the Chen family.

Although her father did not exert any undue pressure, he did ask Lily and her cousins to commit some time to the business after they finished their college educations. Somewhat to her surprise, Lily found the work to be both interesting and exciting although full of challenges. She struggled with how to handle the difficulties associated with being the "boss's daughter" and was acutely aware of her lack of a formal business education. Looking ahead, Lily wonders how she will be able to combine a career with marriage, given the pressure in Asian cultures for men to be the breadwinners. For the time being, she is concentrating on completing an MBA and is continuing to gain more experience by working in different divisions of the family business.

Our family business is now about 20 years old but it's only in the last few years that it's become really successful. My dad started the company after he emigrated here in the late 1970s. He tried his hand at a few other things but then got into baby supplies. At first, it was only manufacturing, but then the retail aspect developed since my uncles were in the same line of business and they helped build a network of connections together. While my uncles continue to be active in various aspects of the business, the ownership of the brand is privately held by my father. Recently, we introduced a line of crib accessories that's doing great and we're thinking of getting into Arts and Crafts style nursery furniture next year.

The idea that Lily might one day take an ownership role in the family business is something that never occurred to her during her formative years.

I never expected that I might be a successor to the business, and in fact, I had no exposure to the business at all until I finished college. I had a pretty standard middle-class background, although I must say my dad was (and still is!) a total workaholic and sometimes we'd hardly see him for days on end. Whenever our family got together, the talk was always about business. A typical conversation among my dad and his brothers would be "What's the competition doing?", "What's selling?", "What isn't selling?" and so on.

I pretty much tuned out all that talk and, when I went to college, I majored in the humanities and took a lot of courses in art history – not exactly a typical foundation for a business career!

In retrospect, I think my liberal arts route did help me to think critically and gave me a broader perspective, but I would probably have had a lot more confidence entering a management position if I had taken some business courses.

Lily credits her father for not exerting pressure on her or her cousins to enter the family business.

My father is quite unusual for someone from his background in that he thinks everyone should be free to go out and pursue his or her own goals. If the business fits in with those goals, then so much the better, but he doesn't believe people should be forced to do anything out of a sense of obligation or duty.

I suppose another reason my father didn't have any expectations of the next generation is that he never had the time to develop any long-term strategy regarding succession. He was just consumed with day-to-day operations and growing the business. When he turned 50, though, I think he suddenly realized he wasn't going to be able to stay in charge forever and that's when he started to get more serious about succession planning. He asked my cousins and me to spend some time in the business after each of us finished college. I'm sure he was hoping we would make a long-term commitment but he made us feel we were simply getting a chance to see if we liked it or not.

At the present time, there are only two members of the next generation of the Chen family working in the family business.

My dad has four brothers, and altogether there are 20 cousins – at least, I think that number is correct! We're a very close-knit group and see each other often. Our family get-togethers are quite something – lots of crazy stories and an insane amount of food. My cousin, John, is the oldest male in my generation (although he's still under 30) and he's the only one to express any kind of interest in working for the business. Some of my other cousins have done short-term internships – and other family members have spent brief periods of time in the business – but it is really only my cousin and me who are currently active.

Despite the fact that the majority of family members are not involved in the business, there is a sense that it has shaped our family and we all feel sentimentally attached to it. In a way I suppose our business has become sort of a beacon of first-generation immigrant success. There's a strong family ethos running through the company and I don't think any of us would be happy if the business just got sold one day. It is definitely a privilege to be part of the business. Our employees' lives are improved economically through the employment we provide and our customers seem to really like our products.

Despite the fact that Lily never intended to work for the family business, she has been pleasantly surprised by the experience.

When my dad asked me to spend some time working for him, I never knew I would get to love the business as much as I do. At this point, I really enjoy working with the great people we have. They're so devoted and loyal to the family and the business. I'd have to say these feelings were a surprise to me and it wasn't until about two years ago that I realized I felt totally committed to the business and that it was something I felt passionate about. It certainly wasn't an automatic "This is what I want to do with my life" kind of feeling. During my early days with the firm, I really appreciated that my father had a measured approach to the whole process and never put any pressure on me or made me feel under some kind of obligation.

Lily has now been working for the family business for four years and has embarked on a conscious plan of trying to gain experience in a variety of areas.

My uncle does retail while we do wholesale and his business is managed in a similar fashion to our company. I started by working with my uncle's company and was given responsibility for the promotion and marketing of one of his lines. My father thought that working for my uncle would be a good opportunity for me to get my feet wet without attracting the attention I would get as the boss's daughter. From my point of view, another advantage was that my uncle's company was still in its formative stages and needed "all hands on deck." The relative lack of hierarchy meant that everyone was expected to pitch in and do whatever was required. For example, if a local store needed new product, the head of operations might be the one to deliver it. The work was not always glamorous, but I got firsthand experience in all aspects of running the business. Personally, I think that entry-level work is invaluable for any successor because it inspires respect for the organization, its people and its processes. Without it, I don't think I would have been able to define my working style and establish my expectations.

When I transitioned over to my father's company – which is larger and has a more sophisticated structure – things didn't work out too well. I was named to a senior vice president position after my first month on the job! I was not accustomed to the level of deference this created because I still saw myself as an active trainee. In addition, I can see that the title itself created a lot of distance between me and the teams I led. The expectation was that I would just attend meetings and sort of learn through osmosis. I felt quite uncomfortable in that situation. Not only am I a very hands-on person, but I also have an entrepreneurial streak of my own. I had to go back to management and plead my case. Essentially, I told them I was in it for the long haul and that I wasn't going to be happy with some empty executive title.

To tell you the truth, I actually thought that attending meetings would be a good way to learn. However, it didn't take me too long to figure out that I needed to educate myself from the ground up and that it was in my own best interests to argue myself back down through the organization.

Lily quickly realized that a lack of formal business training was a serious impediment to her progress.

My family has always had a strong entrepreneurial tradition and the focus has never been on achieving academic success. In fact, I sense that my dad and his brothers tend to pride themselves on the way they learned by doing. At any rate, no one ever suggested to me that I take some courses in business or finance before I joined the firm. Consequently, I've been forced to play catch-up. It was quite embarrassing to be sitting in a meeting and to realize I was the only person who couldn't read the financials. It is so important to be able to understand the numbers and be able to tell a story from the numbers. I started taking continuing education classes and, by the end of next year, I will have completed a distance learning MBA degree.

Two years after starting with the family firm, Lily joined its head office. In many respects, she welcomed the move because of the new challenges it presented. However, one challenge she could do without is the attention she attracts as the boss's daughter.

Currently, I'm working as a strategist in our product planning division. I'm concerned with long-range planning and working on strategies for taking new products to the market. On the very first day I joined the head office, I had a difficult moment with a co-worker who said, "I'm not treating you with kid gloves just because you're the boss's daughter." He was typical of the people I would meet who were pre-emptively antagonistic as a result of my role. On the other hand, some people just acquiesce to any decision that you make – because of your position – and that's not right, either. I realized I had to adapt and find my own performance indicators and not allow extraneous factors to inhibit my work and the interaction with my teams. That antagonistic co-worker and I now enjoy a good working relationship, but it has taken some effort to get to this point.

Initially, I tried hard to position myself so I wasn't treated any differently than anyone else but, the harder I tried, the more I realized I couldn't deny who I was. The fact that I was uncomfortable certainly inhibited my work. It also made learning more difficult. Some people dismissed the idea that I was genuinely excited to learn from them while others were overeager to contribute to my training without any realistic sense of pacing.

I am still a junior in most team meetings but there is a certain sort of immunity in my position. I just have to accept that I am either taken too seriously or else my ideas are just pushed under the table. I think I'm finally becoming more comfortable with my role and the different ways in which I am perceived. For the next couple of years, I'm planning on joining one of the production and development teams to gain more experience on the front lines. I hope that when it's time for me to join the general management team I will be much more confident in my abilities, and the fact I am the boss's daughter will become a non-issue.

Looking ahead to the time when she is part of the general management team, Lily believes that her first priority will be implementing a succession plan.

Transitioning the business from my father's generation to my generation is going to be a huge challenge. In the past, the pressure of running and growing the business has meant that any time the subject of succession was introduced, it would always end up being tabled. Fortunately, or unfortunately, we haven't had any major conflict situation that would have led to the implementation of more formalized governance procedures. Right now the business is a classic entrepreneurially driven model. We need to find a way to bring in a sustainable management team, and cover everything from daily operations to financial strategy to general management controls. Some effort has already been made to come up with more formal management processes, which is obviously a key component in continuity planning for the business.

We have also done some preliminary work by meeting with professionals to go over basic planning strategies – a kind of "Succession Planning 101." We have learned about estate planning and trusts and familiarized ourselves with tax-efficient transfers.

The further you get into it, the more complicated it becomes. From our employees' point of view, I'm sure they simplify the process by thinking, "First he is the owner; then she is the owner." But we've looked into all sorts of possible options from shared ownership to multiple family ownership. We've also looked into employee stock ownership plans and the possibility of making an initial public offering.

My dad and uncles have put a lot of the responsibility for this research on my shoulders. In fact, I've finally come to the conclusion it's up to me to figure out this whole sticky thing called succession. They are very open to the ideas and research that I bring to the table, but I don't get the sense they have the time or the will to take control of the process.

Throughout the discussions to date, we've been careful to keep open lines of communication with the extended family. We give them frequent updates on our possible courses of action. I also like to tell them where I am and what I am doing to prepare myself for ownership responsibilities.

Lily clearly wishes to stay on good terms with her extended family, but at the same time, she recognizes she is challenging traditional expectations.

Although the older members of my family have been living here for 30 years, they still see things through an Asian perspective. While they know I'm very involved in the business and that I enjoy it immensely, they probably still think that succession should take place through paternal lines. They're not against my involvement, but they probably don't want me to do any "heavy lifting." They have a strongly defined view of what constitutes a man's domain and what constitutes a woman's. I am the first woman in our family to work outside the home.

Given my upbringing, I do share many of the family's values but I also have a strong drive to perpetuate the business. I don't think these factors are necessarily in opposition. Yes, the paternal aspect was always stressed, but we also received a lot of coaching regarding our social obligation to be self-sufficient, self-sustaining and successful in whatever we did. My hope for the future is that I can work together with my cousin John, and we can complement each other with our unique skill sets. It is harder for him to be fully involved at this point, because he is not a participant in any of our succession discussions. His parents are not owners; therefore, he is coming on board not knowing what his future position in the business will be.

For the time being, Lily is comfortable with the fact that she doesn't know how things will turn out in the long run.

At the present time, I am eager to learn all I can. I'm working hard toward an MBA in the hope that I can make a significant contribution to the family business. Whether I'll be solely in an ownership position or whether I'll be actively involved in a senior management position remains to be seen. A lot of people – mostly outside the family – ask me questions like, "When are you going to take over the business?" Or "What will you do once you're running the show?" I find these are very loaded questions, and they put me in an awkward position.

Luckily, my dad never puts undue pressure on me. If a time ever comes that I'm not enjoying or feeling fulfilled by the business, then my father totally recognizes that I will take a step back. Having said that, there is still some pressure to ensure the succession goes smoothly. My father is actively involved in building a non-family management team so that it's not a disastrous situation if I should decide the business is not a good fit for me.

Looking ahead, I know that I will face some difficult challenges. How hard will it be for me to run a family business while, at the same time, fulfilling my other goals of being a wife and a mother? And how will my future husband react to my position in the business when there is the expectation for the man to be the breadwinner in Asian cultures? I try not to let these concerns distract me from my goal. My dad has always said, "If you want something badly enough, you can always find a way," and I'm enough like him to think that is true.

WHAT THE ADVISORS SAY

Lily brings a fresh approach from the next generation. Recognizing the inevitability of mortality with greater clarity, perhaps, than most of her family, Lily feels a responsibility to get the succession planning process under way for the sake of all.

By her own admission, Lily is not yet ready to take the helm, but she is working hard to acquire the necessary skills and experience. She provides us with a firsthand account of some of the trials that offspring go through when entering the family business.

Given Lily's cultural background and her community's gender role expectations, it would be helpful if her father formally named Lily as his heir apparent. This would have the added benefit of getting management used to the idea while her father is still around to address any challenges or concerns.

NEXT STEPS

FORMALIZING A SUCCESSION PLAN

Lily and her father recognize the need for a formal succession plan covering both ownership and management, and they have taken the first steps towards that end. They should be commended for the measures they have already taken towards formalizing the management process and having some preliminary meetings with professionals.

The lack of a comprehensive plan, however, presents a significant risk to the business and the family. The fact that Lily's father has not dedicated a lot of time to thinking about succession is understandable given his entrepreneurial spirit and the fact that this will be the first transition of ownership of the business. However, as the current owner of the business, Lily's dad needs to make a firm commitment to the process. Because of her youth and her lack of formal business training, it is not appropriate to expect Lily to assume responsibility for the process. Instead, her father should engage the necessary professional help to put a plan in place that will cover all eventualities including whether or not Lily is the ultimate successor.

REVIEWING THE OPTIONS

Lily mentions that the family has considered ESOPs and an IPO as possible exit strategies. While those vehicles certainly are options, they should not necessarily be considered frontrunners. The level of operational complexity that arises in either of those options can be onerous. In addition, liquidity for the controlling shareholders after an IPO is seriously limited due to the potential impact on the public markets. Other paths to consider may include a simple re-capitalization or partial sale of the business.

SUCCESSOR DEVELOPMENT PLAN

Lily has tried her best to get a start in the business by learning from the ground up. In most cases, that is the approach that works best. Learning about the business from as many vantage points as possible will not only broaden Lily's business experience but will help her be a better manager in the future. In addition, Lily's intention of working towards the completion of her MBA is the right approach and will go a long way towards filling the gaps in her formal business education. In addition, Lily may want to get involved in industry groups or programs beyond her formal studies.

5

ONE BIG HAPPY FAMILY

Chuck Lawson was originally not interested in working for the family business, but he can now look back on an involvement lasting more than 40 years. Currently, there are five members of the third generation of the Lawson family working in the business, together with seven people from the fourth generation.

Chuck's father and uncle founded the business in the late 1950s, together with the father-in-law of Chuck's uncle. This makes Chuck technically third generation. Originally, the firm concentrated on the manufacture of fire sprinkler systems for industrial and commercial applications, but over the years the product range has expanded to air-monitoring devices, smoke detectors, and emergency and safety lighting. Annual sales are currently in excess of $160 million.

Currently, none of the founders is involved in the running of the firm. Chuck's oldest brother is legally and technically the firm's president, but the Lawson family essentially operates the business through an executive committee comprised of seven family members. This somewhat unusual arrangement has evolved over time and seems to offer a very effective mechanism for incorporating successive generations into the management of the business.

I graduated from college in 1967 with a major in mathematics. My intention was to accept a job that had been offered to me in systems analysis. It would have meant a move to New York City, which was a pretty big deal for me as a young guy. My dad, however, had other plans for me. In fact, he said he was going to break my arms and legs if I didn't join the family business!

I had never seriously thought of joining the firm. It was quite small at that time and only operated in Indiana. I couldn't envision what role I could play that would both challenge me and add value at the same time. The last thing I wanted was to work for the family firm and just be a part of the scenery. In the end, I turned down the job in New York City and went into the business, although I have to say I had a lot of misgivings.

Chuck's first hands-on experience with the family business was working in sales.

I came on board at the same time as my younger brother, and we were told to start selling the product. Since the company was so small, there was actually nothing else to do. At the time, there were five of us in sales – myself, my two brothers and my two cousins (my uncle's sons). We learned about the business by selling the product and pretty soon we started to get good at it and landed some big accounts. It didn't hurt that we were in friendly competition with each other. I know I was certainly putting in long hours. I remember one day when I was on the phone and surrounded by piles of paper and my dad walked over and asked, "Are you still worried about not having enough to do?" As the company grew, of course, there were many more responsibilities to take on and many more opportunities outside of sales.

The last of my siblings to come into the business was my sister, who is 14 years younger than I am. She successfully created her own niche by coming up with the idea of focusing on the retail/ consumer market – carbon monoxide detectors and smoke alarms for household use. I think it's fair to say that all of us have been able to make useful contributions in our own distinct ways.

When Chuck entered the business, his father and uncle occupied the roles of chief executive officer and chief operating officer.

My uncle's father-in-law was pretty much taking a back seat by the time I came on board and, a few years later, he was bought out and left the business. Sadly, my dad passed away 14 years ago but my uncle, at the age of 90, was still coming into the office until last year when he formally relinquished the title of president. He would come in and walk around and talk to everybody. But, since then, his health has taken a turn for the worse.

Both my dad and my uncle were active until they weren't able to work anymore. The idea of retirement never seemed to enter their heads! Over time, they simply did less and less and the younger generation took over the workload. When you are instrumental in starting a company, I guess it is hard to turn your back on your baby. Now my older brother is officially the company president, but we choose not to use titles in our day-to-day operations.

Chuck and his family have elected to run the company through an executive committee with membership drawn from each generation.

When my father and uncle were still active, they came up with the idea of enlisting an executive committee to run the company. The original committee was comprised of my father, my uncle, myself, my two brothers, and my two cousins. Membership grew to eight people when my sister joined the company a number of years later.

As my dad and uncle reduced their active involvement, the third generation took more of a leadership role on the committee. About five years ago, one of my cousins wanted to go his own way so his shares were bought out. Around that time, we added two members

*of the fourth generation to the executive committee. Currently, we
have seven members. We meet twice a week over lunch.*

Chuck readily admits that there wasn't a lot of planning behind the
establishment and operation of the executive committee.

*The executive committee idea seemed like the right approach at
the time, and it has just evolved as the company has evolved.
The big advantage for our family is that the next generation is
brought in on a level playing field with the older generation. It
operates on the basis of "one person, one vote," although most
of the time we don't vote. We prefer to talk our way through the
issues and arrive at a consensus. The third and fourth generations are equal participants and have equal voices, so the whole
idea of seniority is out the window. It's obvious that we operate
quite differently than the majority of companies, but the system
works for us and we plan on sticking with it.*

*We have been lucky in that we have never faced any major
conflicts and are usually able to achieve a consensus. On the
rare occasions that we can't, it's one person, one vote and the
majority wins. In 25 years, we have probably had only a hand-
ful of situations where we needed a vote to resolve an issue.*

Chuck is quick to point out that this degree of family harmony is
not simply a matter of good fortune.

*We have been very proactive in developing and implementing
family governance policies including employment policies, the
development of a mission statement and the establishment of
a family council. Our employment policy, for example, clearly
stipulates that a family member wishing to enter the business is
required to work elsewhere for at least two years and there has to
be a real job for that person and not some fabricated position.*

We also have a policy regarding in-laws. We do not employ in-laws, period. I think the lack of conflict between family members can most definitely be attributed to the fact that we have not only created family governance policies, but we also abide by them.

Our executive committee is also governed by rules such as members being required to step down at the age of 65. We enforced that policy with regard to my older brother and, since I will be 65 in a year's time, I will most likely also be stepping down at that time. According to our rules, committee approval is required for any member to stay on the executive committee past the age of 65.

For years, we had a simple buy/sell agreement in place, but my cousin is the only family member who has sold since the early days of the company. In his situation, we didn't really use the agreement, we simply negotiated a price and that was it. At the current time, we are working on the development of a more formal policy with valuations every year or two and a set price established for the selling of shares. We also want to address the question of which family members have the first right to buy the shares – your siblings, your cousins, etc. In the event that no family member wishes to purchase the shares, then we want to stipulate that the company will buy them.

The Lawson family has also worked closely with a family business consultant over the last ten years as a way of anticipating and mediating conflict.

Before my cousin sold his shares a few years ago, there were concerns that we would potentially have too many members of the fourth generation wanting to work in the business at the same time. At that time, the company was smaller than it is today and there was a lot of uncertainty about how we would handle the numbers. We were working on this potential problem with our consultant when my cousin made the decision that he would leave. His departure took three potential fourth generation family members out of the mix so the cloud of uncertainty that hung over the future lifted. At this point, all of the fourth generation who are actively involved in the business are working well with the third generation so, through a combination of circumstances, we are making a relatively seamless transition.

The creation of an outside board of advisors has also helped the Lawson family navigate through some sensitive family situations.

We're just like any other family – sometimes there are situations in which feelings get hurt. For example, someone's child gets to sit on the executive committee and another's does not. In order to bring some objectivity to these judgment calls, we have formed an outside advisory board. We developed criteria for the selection of advisory board members. For example, members have to be people not previously known by us, and they have to have experience at the level of vice president or beyond.

There are three advisors on the board and they meet with our executive committee three times a year. Even though the board doesn't have any real power, the advisors have been extremely useful in helping us see things objectively. For instance, they helped us come up with the rule that executive committee members should step down when they reach 65. It could be hard for an executive committee member in his 60s to come up with that rule but for the ongoing welfare of the business, it's the right rule.

In addition to the executive committee and the advisory board, the Lawson family also has a number of other formal structures in place.

Once a quarter, we have an active owners meeting that includes all of the shareholders who are currently active in the business (12 in number) plus the non-active shareholders. My daughter, for example, is not able to come into the business due to family obligations, but she is a shareholder and the same holds true for one of my cousin's sons. We hold a lunch meeting and bring everyone up to date on developments and provide a forum for questions and answers.

We also have a family council in which all family members, including spouses, participate. In order to attend, you have to be 21 years of age. I think these meetings are a great way to get the next generation involved. We give them status reports and financial reports and they can get a good idea of how we operate and how they might be able to contribute.

For many years, the Lawson family went about succession planning on a somewhat informal basis.

Like any other firm, we had our meetings with lawyers and accountants about passing on shares and limiting our tax exposure. We didn't, however, spend a lot of time thinking about governance and this is an area we are still working on. We attended a succession planning seminar put on by our bank about 20 years ago, which came at a very opportune time. We were beginning to see the future participation of the fourth generation and realized we needed to be proactive in putting policies in place to manage family involvement and establish standards and expectations.

Following the seminar with the bank, we joined a family business advisory group and have learned a lot from the owners of other family businesses. Communication is such a powerful tool! We talk out our issues and have discussions about a wide range of topics. Usually, we don't have set topics but instead we tackle issues as they arise.

Chuck is happy the business has been kept in the family and has provided employment for so many family members.

Everyone wants to keep the business in the family. It keeps the family together and it's nice that we all get along. As long as the business makes money, it also provides a comfortable living for the family.

In our family, the thing to do is to come into the business. All the kids have grown up around it, and they just naturally gravitate to it as a place to work. I think it's great that all of the fourth generation came into the business without any pressure to do so.

As the business continues to grow, we will have to address at some point the issue of more non-family involvement. In the last few years, we have hired a lot more non-family managers, but none of them are on the executive committee. Eventually, we will have to decide, as a team, when – or if – we will allow non-family members to be part of the executive committee. Clearly, we are in the process of migrating from a more informal family operation to a more formalized business. We have always tried to put the business first but, let's face it, it's impossible for a family to always be 100 percent business first.

Nepotism is a subject that frequently comes up in discussions of family businesses. I have to say it's how I got my job so how can I be against it? Seriously, I do understand that employees might be concerned about their positions being taken by family members. On the other hand, many employees like many of the other aspects of being employed by a family business. We tend to have a friendly kind of atmosphere, we treat everyone somewhat like extended family and we provide good benefits. Most important, we are here to stay, so there is good job security. I'm sure there have been times when a family member got some advantage over a non-family member, but you have to look at the whole picture, and I'm sure that is what our non-family employees do.

Overall, I think you have to separate the business component from the family component. The business has succeeded because we have the right products at the right prices. The family has done well because we have figured out a way to get the job done, keep conflict to a minimum and have some fun along the way. What more can you ask for?

WHAT THE ADVISORS SAY

Chuck Lawson and his extended family have clearly taken time from day-to-day concerns to address the many issues surrounding succession planning. With the help of independent advisors, they have reached agreement on family governance and employment policies and are well on their way to implementing succession policies for family members. Adherence to the principles of carefully crafted family governance documents is not only good business, but it also helps avoid favoritism, hurt feelings and rivalries between different branches of the family. The Lawsons have developed a somewhat unusual management approach, but the inter-generational structure of their executive committee is obviously working to their advantage.

NEXT STEPS

INCENTIVES FOR NON-FAMILY MANAGEMENT

The Lawson family business has a heavy concentration of family members active in both ownership and management. Given these circumstances, the family would be well advised to establish incentives to both attract non-family key executives and ensure that they stay with the company once hired. The most significant way of generating loyalty to the company is by offering meaningful economic participation in its long-term success.

DIVERSIFICATION OF ASSETS

Over the course of just a few generations, this family business has progressed from start-up to significant entity with multiple constituencies. At this stage, it is important that the family considers diversifying its financial interests. The next logical step may be the creation of a family office to facilitate the centralized management of affairs. A family office could support the longevity of the business, handle the investment of unrelated family wealth, act as a means of facilitating the transfer of shares and represent disparate family interests fairly.

ADDRESSING THE LAW OF LARGE NUMBERS

Once the participation in the ownership of a business gets to 6+ family groups, there is a real risk of the law of large numbers coming into play. Multiple representation makes it increasingly difficult to keep the family together and can create serious impediments to running the business effectively. Clearly, the formalization of the buy/sell arrangements the family is currently undertaking will aid in minimizing conflict. However, there should be additional focus on a funding mechanism to meet the liquidity needs that can arise from multiple redemptions.

6

FIRST YOU BUILD, THEN YOU SELL

Since moving to the Los Angeles area some 30 years ago, Murray Prentice has bought and sold more than ten businesses. He is also an investor in a number of private equity funds. At one time, he was the owner of a property development company and a couple of motels. He liquidated his interests in those businesses and moved on to his next entrepreneurial challenge.

Currently, his main interest is a large printing operation, but he also owns a graphic design studio, a specialty photo processing plant and an advertising agency. At one point, he decided to locate a number of his businesses in a warehouse area with promising real estate potential. Unfortunately, it lacked any conveniently located restaurants for his employees. Murray was able to solve that problem by opening a gourmet sandwich and latte bar that proved so popular it is now part of a chain of 15.

Clearly, Murray enjoys the process of building something from nothing but, unlike the owners of many businesses, he has no qualms about selling and moving on.

Murray has three children, but the last thing on his mind is build-ing a mini-empire for them. In his experience, bringing children into a family business is detrimental both to the business and to the owner's relationship with his or her children.

My guiding principle is, "First you build, then you sell, and you never pass the business on to the family." I made a lot of money when I sold my first group of businesses and that provided the capital for my next investment. When I sold, people would always question me and ask why my kids hadn't wanted to enter the business. I never intended to bring my children into the business, but people always seem surprised when I tell them that.

Murray has a number of reasons why he is against bringing children into a business.

First, I always think the nicest relationship you have is with your children. Why ruin it by being in business together?

Second, as the boss and the dad, I think it's very hard to avoid the Peter Principle of promoting them beyond the level of their capabilities. I've always thought you should help your kids achieve their maximum potential within the realm of their capabilities. When you start pushing beyond that, it has to be bad for both them and the business.

Third, I think it's very hard on the kids. When they're coming up through the organization, they're always going to be looked at as the boss's son or daughter. Not having any true peers or colleagues can be a very isolating experience.

Finally, I have personally seen a number of family business failures that didn't need to happen. When someone is doing something that isn't the right fit for them and they fail, it's very sad to see their credibility and self-confidence being undermined. The cost to the family as a whole can be huge. Even if the fit is right for them, there's any number of reasons why a business can fail. When you add in the pressures of the family situation, it just compounds the problems.

Murray has very open communication with his children, and they are completely aware of his strong opinions on the subject.

My children know where I stand; we have always discussed these matters very candidly. We don't have formal family meetings, but when we get together over dinner, or whatever, I make them aware of my plans and go through my thought process. My primary motivation is to minimize taxes and, because I am divorced, the last thing I want to create is a huge cash estate that will be liable for a big tax hit.

While Murray is opposed to bringing his children into his businesses, he is certainly not averse to helping them in a monetary way.

Ever since the children were young, I have been buying them different stocks for their birthdays. Actually, it's one of my great personal weaknesses! If I see a good buy, I just can't resist.

I've always thought it's important for children to be aware of the idea of investments from a young age so that they have an understanding of how the business world works. I have introduced my children to people in the financial realm whom I respect, and I hope the early exposure serves them well.

I am involved in a number of private equity funds and my children know the people who handle my assets. I pass on a lot of information to my kids, but as far as I'm concerned, what's really critical is that they have sound individuals to advise them.

Some people think they can manage a substantial amount of money themselves, but I know otherwise – you have to go to the experts. At this point, I believe my children understand this, and I feel quite comfortable that they will be able to handle their wealth.

Murray's appreciation of the value of expert assistance has been the touchstone of his career as a venture capitalist.

I do not have the responsibility for day-to-day operations in any of the companies I own. Instead, I prefer the role of chairman of the board, and I select the people I want to run the business. I know there are people out there who can do a way better job than I ever could, so why wouldn't I hire the best person? That's the key to building value, as far as I'm concerned. Any successful owner should recognize the need to delegate, but some people lack the intellectual maturity to let go of the reins.

I've always thought that Henry Ford had the right idea. He knew he wasn't the brightest guy in the world, and he also liked to play around and have a good time. His solution was to hire the best people he could find and the rest is history.

Now that he is in his mid-60s, Murray has become more concerned with winding down his affairs.

I have a planned exit, but the timing depends on achieving certain financial milestones I have set. One of the businesses will be sold in the next two years since the other shareholders would like to realize their investment. With regard to the others, once we have achieved significant growth and then hit a plateau, it will be time to sell. I have a couple of other businesses that are on 5–10 year holds, but we need to jump-start sales to make some real money. By my mid-70s, all my businesses will probably be sold.

From an estate planning perspective, I have optimized my use of trusts and other vehicles that enable you to move money to others while minimizing exposure to taxes. That's been my aim — to end up with the lowest possible tax payable upon my death. I don't know why they call it an inheritance tax. It's a death tax because you have to pay this money to die!

Like many successful business owners, Murray has given a lot of thought to the legacy that he wishes to leave for future generations.

Naturally, I want my family members to be looked after. However, I have really struggled with what is an appropriate amount for an inheritance. I don't want to give an amount where the money creates a negative influence on the lives of my children. At first, I decided to allow my kids a $5 million inheritance, but as they matured, I decided to double that. I'm quite certain each of them could handle that kind of wealth, but then I ask myself, what about their children? In deciding how much to give, I don't think there are any hard-and-fast rules. You have to take the individuals and their personalities into consideration. I have come to the point where I think my children will do well with their wealth, thanks to their values and their upbringing.

Apart from helping out my kids, I also want to give back to society since, it has given me so much. Education is very important to me, as is medical research, and I plan to do more in those areas during my retirement. It would be nice to set up some kind of foundation and leave a lasting legacy.

WHAT THE ADVISORS SAY

Murray has approached the succession issue from a different standpoint than most business owners. He has always been averse to employing family members and does not wish to pass on his business to his heirs. However, Murray is certainly not against keeping his wealth in the family, and to that end has taken steps to ensure his children are prepared to properly manage their inheritance. Given appropriate tax and estate planning, Murray's immediate heirs may enjoy the maximum economic benefit without the risks that are often associated with inheriting a family business.

Like many successful owners, Murray has struggled with the issue of determining an appropriate amount to bequeath his children. While feeling his children are capable of handling their inheritance, Murray cannot help but ponder the possible negative effects of inherited wealth on future generations of the family.

Murray's story is a clear illustration of the fact that there is no single "right" approach to succession planning. For some owners, keeping the business in the family is a major objective while for others, like Murray, ownership is merely a means to an end.

NEXT STEPS

RECONSIDERING EXIT TIMETABLE

Murray has been systematically reducing his day-to-day involvement in his various business holdings and is planning for the day when he can continue to gain wealth by assuming a more passive investor role.

However, Murray should possibly revisit his phased exit timetable. By his own account, he expects to still be maintaining ownership of some of his businesses into his mid-70s. While Murray currently enjoys good health, it would be imprudent not to consider the effect of disability or death on these plans, and to act to protect his investment.

SHARING THE WEALTH

Many people in Murray's position struggle with the issue of how best to share their wealth. Having ensured the financial well-being of his children, Murray can now invest time and money in meeting his philanthropic goals by establishing charitable trusts or foundations in the fields of education and medical research. Seeking expert advice in tax and estate planning will assist Murray in maximizing the value of these givings.

Becoming involved in the activities of a philanthropic endeavor will also provide Murray with a suitable outlet for his considerable energies as he winds down his business activities.

FURTHER EDUCATION

Murray has done a good job of informally teaching his children the broad principles of investing and the importance of money managers. However, the achievement of a higher level of financial fluency and investment knowledge will be required to best preserve the wealth for future generations. Murray's children would be well advised to seek more education to that end.

7

KEEPING ON TRACK

Thomas Carlisle is a living example of the American dream. Descended from a great-grandfather who arrived as a penniless immigrant and ended up making his fortune in the railroad business, Thomas and his siblings are now preparing to pass on the family wealth dynasty to the fifth generation. Over the years, the story of the Carlisle family has not been one of extravagant high living. Instead, the emphasis has been on conservation of assets, prudent diversification and a conscious commitment to stewardship of resources. A significant portion of its accumulated wealth has also been channeled into a private family foundation that supports a wide range of philanthropic activities.

> *Our family company was started almost 120 years ago by my great-grandfather, Andrew. He was born into a large family in Scotland, and as the second youngest, was pretty far down in the pecking order. There was precious little opportunity for young men of his generation, so like many of his contemporaries, he left in search of his fortune. I've never quite understood how he managed to work his way up in the world. It was probably a combination of being in the right place at the right time and being prepared to work extremely hard. From a few surviving letters we do know that he was fascinated by the railroad and excited by the way it was opening up the country.*

Buoyed by the success of his original investment in the railroad, Andrew Carlisle was quick to exploit other possibilities that presented themselves.

My great-grandfather was very business minded and had a lot of savvy. He could see that once you built a track and got a service running, there would be a need for hotels, food provisioning, laundry services, building construction and so on. It was a bad day for him if he hadn't had a good idea before lunch! Right from the start, he realized that diversification was the key to long-term profitability and he succeeded in growing the company tremendously.

The principle of diversification is one that continues to guide the company to the present day.

By the time my grandfather took over the company, the writing was already on the wall so far as the railroads were concerned. Over the years, we've been involved in many kinds of businesses – manufacturing, insurance, real estate and development. The whole point is to always be on the lookout for new opportunities while, at the same time, managing your exposure to risk.

The current owners are fourth generation and are preparing to keep the business in the family by handing it over to the fifth generation – an impressive achievement.

My grandfather had two sons and his brother had four daughters. My grandfather saw a lot of potential conflict in this situation, and he decided to buy out his brother's interest. As a result, that branch of the family has an investment portfolio and real estate holdings rather than stock in the company.

My grandfather's two sons – my dad and uncle – entered the business at a time when we were heavily involved in various manufacturing enterprises. This was long before foreign labor markets were seriously undercutting U.S. manufacturing and we benefited from increasing demand for consumer products.

*Unfortunately, my uncle passed away suddenly, at quite a
young age, and all of his estate went to my dad. This left my
dad as the only member of the third generation to be involved
in the business.*

*My father decided to sell a number of the manufacturing subsid-
iaries, and it was then that my sister and I entered the business.
We had a very significant infusion of liquidity from the sale and
used it to increase our real estate holdings and private equity
investments. Our older brother is an inactive shareholder who
sits on the board. My siblings and I are all in our mid- to late-40s
so it is certainly not too soon to start thinking about how we will
pass on the business to the fifth generation.*

Despite the tradition established by previous generations, Thomas
was not always sure that he would become an active participant in
the family business.

*My dad is a big believer in gaining experience before coming on
board – either working for the firm at a distant location or working outside the business altogether. My father encouraged all of
us kids to go to college away from our home state and I think we
all got a lot out of that change of scenery. As for myself, I was
finishing up my college degree at the same time I was starting
a career in banking. I could easily have gone in that direction.
However, I think my dad really wanted to have me work in the
business, and he made me an offer that was too good to resist.*

While Thomas and his sister have effectively taken over the running of the business, their father continues to exert some influence.

*Dad is officially retired now, but he still chairs our board
and manages some of the family trusts. At the age of 71, he
is removed from the day-to-day operations, but he still has an*

administrative assistant, still comes into the office every day and still calls me for a daily update on what's going on. It's easy to feel resentful, but I try to put myself in his shoes. It's not like he doesn't trust us to run the company. It's more that he has a hard time letting go. The business was such a huge part of his life, and he hasn't found an interest to take its place.

Thomas acknowledges that some form of conflict is inevitable in a family-run business.

My sister and I had a minor run-in when our father named me president seven years ago. At the time, she definitely had a "why not me?" attitude. We've sort of gotten over that by now, but we're still competitive. We each have our own pet projects, and there's always the issue of how much gets allocated to each project. The reality of our life working together is that I am involved in her business and she is involved in mine! Fortunately, all our conflicts have been amicably resolved. Our interests are aligned and there are no fundamental differences of opinion. As a family, we all see the value in meeting our financial goals and achieving our benchmarks.

Formalizing these shared values in the form of a family constitution has become a priority for the Carlisles.

We've hired a consultant to work with us on developing a family constitution. I think my sister and I are more closely in agreement as to how we would like the family governance to be structured while my brother is more free-spirited. We need to come to some consensus, and so we have gone to our dad and asked him to provide some leadership in this area.

What's motivating us is we all feel it's important to keep the business in the family. We share a sense of responsibility that it's up to us to keep the tradition going. It's almost like the business is our vocation.

Overhauling the board structure is one way in which Thomas hopes to improve operating efficiency and address the issue of accommodating both active and inactive shareholders.

Currently, my brother – an inactive shareholder – sits on the board together with other members who are family or friends. The board is the way we try to keep shareholders informed. It's more of an educational forum than anything else. We produce a semi-annual report to shareholders that we try to make as comprehensive as possible. My brother has a good overall grasp of the business, but he is not engaged in the nitty-gritty decision making process. Since there are things we do that affect him, we try to make sure he is kept fully informed.

My sister and I both feel that changing the board structure would allow us to operate much more efficiently than we do right now. We would like to have two boards operating at different levels. The first, more company-related board, would be used for strategy building. It would handle questions regarding specific investments such as whether or not we should be in a particular class of real estate. This board would, in turn, report to a family office board. My brother and other inactive family associates would be able to oversee more general matters such as asset allocation and return on investments. We are very conscious of the fact that the business provides a significant investment vehicle for a number of family members, and that is why performance is so important. Having good communication and transparency with family members and other people who have a vested interest in the business is something we strive very hard to achieve.

The concept of preservation of wealth has been instilled into each successive generation of the Carlisle family – and Thomas and his sister are no exception to this rule.

We've just developed a five-year strategic plan and have established financial goals and benchmarks. In 25 years, we want to triple the family's net worth. In looking towards the future, we have run through various Monte Carlo simulations and have taken a look at a variety of iterations. In our projections, we used the year 2025 as a likely date by which my sister and I would be ready to retire. Neither of us has set a specific goal of when we will check out. I think a lot will depend on health and family interests.

By 2025, my eldest daughter (who is the first born of the fifth generation) will be in her 30s. My sister's youngest child will be 24, so all the cousins will be at, or approaching, an age where they would be ready to make a contribution to the business.

Preparing the fifth generation to carry on the family business is an important part of the succession process.

We hope to develop programs for the fifth generation to educate them on the history of the company and the family. My sister and I also feel very strongly that they need to learn about the responsibilities that come along with wealth and ownership. Restraint is not something that comes easily to young people, but I think it has been key to the continuing success of our family. We have spending policies that hover around 1.5 percent to 2 percent of our net worth and we really monitor our consumption. I think we grew up with a very conservative approach to managing our wealth – limit consumption, minimize taxes and capital losses and make sound investments.

We have been fortunate enough to receive the legacy of three generations before us. Now it's our watch, and we have a duty to preserve this legacy and hand it on to the next generation.

If we don't raise responsible children and we don't take on the responsibility of preparing the business for the next generation, then I believe we have to ask ourselves if we are really doing our jobs.

Philanthropy is an important means of discharging the responsibilities that come with a legacy of wealth.

For the last 25 years, we have had a private family foundation that supports a wide range of philanthropic activities. Typically, the foundation is funded through the estates of deceased family members. Over time, we have significantly grown the value of the foundation through strategic investments. I like to think that our philanthropic goals are working to benefit future generations. Just the other day, in fact, my youngest daughter expressed her interest in preventing animal cruelty. I hope she will get involved with the foundation and pursue the causes that are important to her.

Looking to the future comes very naturally to someone in Thomas Carlisle's position.

When you are in the fourth generation, succession is something you always think about. Our goal is to try and keep the family and our interests together. We certainly want to create a platform for the next generation to come into the business, but there is absolutely no obligation for them to do so. Our philosophy is that each member of the next generation should be free to pursue something that he or she is passionate about. If that takes them away from working in the business, so be it. You can continue to

*be an owner without being an employee, but naturally we hope
that at least one of our children will be motivated to carry the
business forward to the sixth generation.*

WHAT THE ADVISORS SAY

Thomas is clearly focused on the day-to-day challenges of running
a successful business. At the same time, he has a strong sense of
respect for his forbearers and a keen desire to pass the business on
to the next generation.

While many entrepreneurs find it difficult to focus on planning
for the future, Thomas recognizes that forward thinking has been
the key to preserving and growing the wealth in his family. By the
time a business is in the hands of the fourth generation, succession
planning has obviously been addressed before, and the need to
continue to engage in it is instilled in the owners as a priority.

The Carlisle family business has had the advantage of relatively
tight spans of ownership over the last several generations. In other
words, the law of large numbers has not kicked in and the business
has not had to support multiple families with varied interests. This
situation may very well change as the business transitions into
successive generations. Skillfully addressing the issue of multiple
family involvement will be key to ensuring the continuing success
of the Carlisle family's business operations.

NEXT STEPS

WEALTH PRESERVATION

The family would benefit from creating policies regarding their
wealth. In particular, there needs to be a clear intra-family understanding between active and inactive members regarding cash

flow distributions, terms of employment and rules for redeeming family members who wish to go their separate ways. As family members disburse and get less connected to the business operations, it is inevitable that calls for liquidity and diversification of investments will arise. In addition, the family needs to identify a shared mission for their wealth – one that incorporates their values and ethics and that will unite the family in working toward common goals.

FAMILY EDUCATION

The Carlisles could consider using family meetings to educate the younger generations in wealth management for non-business assets in addition to giving them a view into the business itself. Well-conducted family meetings can provide an ideal forum for family members to share information, concerns and suggestions about the family's operations. The governance structure of many successful families includes both a "family council" and an advisory board for the family.

CONTINGENCY PLANNING

Thomas and his sister have begun planning the transition of the business and identifying likely successors with an exit date of 2025 in mind. It is a fact of life, however, that unexpected events do occur – and financial and management planning should be in place to cover an unplanned exit by, or death of, one or both of the two siblings. As part of its contingency planning, the family would also be well advised to put specific plans and directions in place to ensure the continued operation of the business in addition to the proper management of the family's financial affairs.

8
A BICYCLE BUILT FOR TWO

Tony Sabatine is the third-generation owner of a bicycle business. With manufacturing plants in two states, a significant retail presence and a product line ranging from children's bikes to top-of-the-line racing models, Sabatine Cycles has come a long way from its humble beginnings.

Started by Tony's grandfather in the Depression years, the business has had to respond to a number of challenges along the way. During the past decade, the availability of cheap Chinese imports had led Tony to believe the future of his business was in jeopardy. Recently, however, the high price of gas coupled with environmental concerns has led to a rising demand for good quality, yet affordable, American-made bicycles among those people who wish to trade four wheels for two.

Tony is in his late 60s, and while he still enjoys working, he is looking forward to the time when he will have more freedom to do as he chooses. With two sons in the business, one of whom is president, Tony now occupies the position of chairman of the board. Tony and his wife also have a daughter, but she is not actively involved in the business.

My grandfather started the business in 1932. It must have been quite an act of faith (or craziness) during those hard times. There are lots of stories in the family about how tough it was in the early days. Grandfather couldn't afford to pay wages so my father left grammar school in the eighth grade to work in the business.

In those days, people were worried about food, clothes and shelter — not the latest cellphone or the fanciest shoes.

When Grandfather died, his sons were left with a large debt and a couple of garage-sized businesses. For a number of years, my father ran the company with his brother, but they didn't get along well and my uncle wanted out. My dad asked me to leave law school and come and work for him because he couldn't run the business on his own. Actually, it was a much smaller business then, but of course, everything is relative. I left law school without any regrets. It's not like I had any huge aspirations to be a lawyer. Since then, I have worked in the business for my entire adult life.

Despite a lack of any prior experience, Tony was quickly immersed in all aspects of the business.

I relied on my father to show me everything at the beginning, and we maintained a close working relationship for many years. As with all growing businesses, things began to get more detailed and complex, and Dad's capacity for handling matters deteriorated as he aged. My father was around for a long time, and he believed he had a duty to come to the office every day to maintain his business. Towards the end though, the business was moving forward too fast for him to continue playing an active day-to-day role, and his time in the office became more socially motivated.

Tony was in his mid-50s before he began to think seriously about transitioning the business.

One day, I realized my interest in continuing to be in the proverbial rat race was diminished. Maybe it's something that happens when you see your sixtieth birthday approaching more quickly than you'd like. You suddenly start thinking you're not going to live forever! I didn't want to suddenly wake up and realize the things I needed to take care of were beyond my capacity to handle.

It occurred to me that I should get going as quickly as possible. If my sons chose not to come in, then I would need time to decide how to transition the business. On the other hand, if they did come in, it would still take a number of years before I could decide whether or not they were capable of running the business. It's an entrepreneurial, "hands-on" kind of business. You have to be able to adjust to changing markets. I knew it would take time to see if they had what it takes.

As he began to engage in the succession planning process, Tony was by no means committed to keeping the business in the family.

Unlike most Italian-Americans, I never felt I had to try to keep the business in the family. For one thing, we have been successful enough that neither my two sons nor I felt like it was our only option. I'm not one of those people who take a great deal of pride in seeing the family name over the door. To be honest, I could just as easily have cashed out as decided to keep going. My approach was to look at the situation objectively, decide what was the smart course of action and not let emotions get in the way of the decision making.

Both of Tony's sons were already established in careers of their own, and while he wished to offer them the opportunity to join the business, he was careful not to exert any pressure on them to do so.

Both of my sons had been to law school and were doing quite well working in large law firms. Essentially, I sat down with them and said we need to think about the business because I am obviously not going to live forever. The way I saw it, we had three choices: either one of the boys could come on board, or two of them or none of them. I made it clear that I was happy with whatever choice they made.

I did try to point out to my sons what advantages I saw in owning a business – most of them financial. Presuming you run the business successfully, there is the security of income and employment, and there are certainly some advantages and perks in operating a privately held business.

Tony realized that having his sons enter the family business would initially place additional demands on his time.

The one thing I had to make clear was that I couldn't have both of them coming in at the same time. With the amount of teaching I would have had to do, I don't see how I could have run the company at the same time. And while I didn't want to absorb them both within a short time frame, I also didn't want them to leave me hanging regarding their intentions. I told them not to wait 10 years if they wanted to come in. My concern was that, if they came in and it turned out badly, we would need sufficient time to exit the business without jeopardizing past achievements.

As it turned out, about a year after these discussions, my eldest son, Joe, came into the business. That would be eight years ago now. George entered the business about two years after his brother.

One of the issues that had to be immediately addressed when Joe and George decided to join the firm was the question of compensation.

When my sons came on board, it wasn't like they were kids right out of school. Even freshly graduated law students receive substantial compensation. I realized I was competing with their current employers' salary and benefits package. I had to pay them what we could afford and hope this would be acceptable, based on what they were making in their previous jobs.

Once Tony's sons settled into management roles and decided they wanted to carry on in the business, the potentially divisive issue of job titles arose.

I don't believe in co-presidencies. I think it's very hard to run a business with two people at the helm. It was a difficult and emotional process for me to select who would ultimately be my direct successor. Actually, the decision itself was quite easy to make since the differing personalities of my two sons clearly dictated that the younger one would be president and the older one wouldn't. The difficult part, as a parent, was communicating to the son who wouldn't be president the reasons why he wasn't being chosen. When it came time to tell him, I sat down with him and he didn't react badly. At the age of 40, he was mature enough to understand why I made the decision I did.

Tony is pleased that his sons have adapted well to their new career paths.

My boys are both smart and they have good social skills. I think they have handled their responsibilities very well. They have both been quite deferential to me and the pre-existing management team. They have not been rash in insisting that things be done their way.

There have been some situations where I have told them they shouldn't do this or that, but I've allowed them to go their own

*way if they felt strongly about it. Some of those situations result-
ed in failures and they certainly learned from the experience.*

*I've gone out of my way to be a good mentor to them, but at
the same time I make a conscious effort not to bring personal or
family issues into the office setting. One exception I make is that
I will brag about my grandchildren any chance I get!*

*My sons each have a more or less equal amount of responsibility,
but their roles are separate, so they are not competing with each
other. They are both enjoying the same level of compensation,
so we have avoided the monetary frustrations that often seem
to come into play in these situations.*

Tony believes his own life experiences helped him avoid costly
mistakes when it came time to bring his sons into the business.

*I came straight into the business without ever working anywhere
else. In retrospect, I wish it had been otherwise. I wanted my boys
to create their own sense of self-worth which they did by going to
law school and having successful careers in their own right.*

*Along the way, I also learned some of the pitfalls associated with
having family members in the business. For many years, I had a
brother-in-law working in the business. His compensation was
totally out of line with his position and his capabilities. It was a
very awkward situation. The reality is we just had to deal with it
and over compensate him. At the time it was very frustrating and
I took away a lot from that experience.*

For the employees of Sabatine Cycles, having the fourth generation
enter the family business was a welcome turn of events.

I'm sure the employees were extremely happy my sons came in. They must have been concerned that all four members of my management team were getting on in age. The blue-collar workers certainly appreciated the fact that there was young blood coming into the business. To them that meant job security and the prospect of long-term involvement.

Tony is still keeping his options open when it comes to his own retirement plans.

I'm in my late 60s, but I still don't have a formal timeline for exiting the business. As chairman of the board, I still have a fair number of responsibilities. I'm often away traveling with my wife, but when I'm in town, I'm at the office, which is a substantial commitment. However, since I'm not tied to any day-to-day duties, I can come in late or leave early. I'm enjoying the fact that I can choose the pace at which I work. In the old days, we didn't have the benefits of technology like cellphones. It seems like there was a lot more stress when you were caught in traffic and trying to be in 12 places at once. In this day and age, there's a lot more technology and this helps you work when and how you choose.

I think I'm like a lot of people who have run their own business: I don't have a lot of outside interests or activities. I don't go around thinking if I only had more time, I would enjoy playing more golf, or whatever. I enjoy the business; I enjoyed taking it to the level it's now at, and I enjoy watching the success my sons are having in taking over the reins. As for the future, I see myself doing pretty much what I am currently doing.

We don't have a functioning board; we just operate with the management team. I am proud of the job I have done in extricating myself from the day-to-day operations and letting them make the decisions themselves.

Two of the senior managers on my team are having a hard time letting go. I'm trying to be deferential towards them but, at the same time, we've been encouraging them to retire. Both of them are working reduced hours but, because of their personality styles, they tend to take over whenever they are in the office. I think I've been too soft-handed with them but that will have to change. As we bring in younger managers, we need to accelerate the departure of the old guard.

For the most part, Tony is satisfied that the transitioning of the family business has not presented any major challenges.

I think I owe a lot of my success to good genes! Fortunately, I am reasonably smart and also a good communicator. These qualities helped me in the planning process. I was able to interest my sons in joining the business and "indoctrinate" them in our operations. It has been a very peaceful transition. We don't have regular family meetings. I sometimes wonder if we should, but we don't.

Early on in the process of my sons joining the business, we engaged the services of a family business consultant. He met with each of the families separately to talk about hopes, expectations, concerns and so on. From my own point of view, I think I was already pretty much aware of the pitfalls that needed to be avoided. The real value of the exercise was that we were looking at the process from an intellectual standpoint and giving it an objective perspective.

The issue of estate planning has proved to be a much more contentious issue.

We are sitting with a substantial percentage of the estate tied up in the company. This presents a problem with respect to our third child, our daughter Norma, who is not in the business. It would be much easier if we had liquidated the business, and I just had a bundle of cash, but that is not the case.

We had a similar problem with my parents' estate. My sister received stock and this was tied to the employment in the company of her husband (the brother-in-law I referred to earlier.)

Given the size of our company and the fact that it is not publicly traded, I didn't want to give stock to my non-working daughter. I feel this dilutes the reward the boys receive through their work by a third. So, as we gifted stocks and set up grants to the boys, I gave my daughter other assets of an equivalent value. Norma was – and is very appreciative, but I do worry about future inequity. The boys will enjoy all the perks of ownership. I'm not sure she has ever considered that if she takes the money and doesn't make it grow, she will be a lot worse off than her brothers.

It bothers me when I think she didn't get 100 cents on the dollar to begin with because the value of her gift was diluted after tax. Hopefully, her financial picture will look just as rosy as theirs years from now. I help her with her investments, but I still agonize over the way I handled this. My wife and I have spent hours talking it over. The bottom line is I don't want to dilute the boys' efforts.

Although Tony could have made things simpler by selling the company and liquidating the proceeds, he is nonetheless pleased that Sabatine Cycles is now in its fourth generation of family ownership.

I like to think I have run the company with integrity and treated our employees fairly. I'm sure my sons will do their best to maintain the family tradition. I sometimes think if my sons had not wanted any part of the business and I had sold the company, I would have been able to distribute the proceeds evenly and life would have been so much easier. On the other hand, I must say I take a lot of pride in watching my sons run the business and wonder what their great-grandfather would think if he could see them now.

WHAT THE ADVISORS SAY

During the last decade, Tony Sabatine has successfully fended off increased competition and has laid the groundwork for the successful transitioning of the family business to the next generation. He is to be commended for allowing sufficient time to make alternative plans should his sons have been unable or unwilling to assume the leadership roles he had in mind for them. Tony has had to make a difficult choice in selecting one son over the other to assume the presidency of the company, but he has been open in communicating his reasons and has tried to balance their respective responsibilities.

NEXT STEPS

ADDRESSING POTENTIAL CONFLICT

Tony has frankly and openly discussed his plans for the future of the business with his sons and daughter. While all the siblings appear to relate well with each other at this time, it is often the case that suppressed issues come to light when the patriarch departs a family business. It would be advisable for the Sabatine family to create an independent board or appoint a trusted third party so as to have the means of resolving potential future conflict. The risk of intra-sibling dissent is considerably reduced when the "rules of engagement" are outlined in advance.

ENSURING EQUAL DISTRIBUTION

People in Tony's situation often struggle with the issue of "fair versus equal" when it comes to passing on assets to the next generation, particularly if some of these children are not actively involved in the family business. Tony wishes to ensure equal distribution of assets to his children yet the value of those various classes of assets may be vastly different at the time the estate is settled. It would be advisable for Tony to work with his estate planners on a continuing basis to review the value of the allocations made to his children, and maintain the desired balance and equality of distribution. An estate plan should be thought of as a living document that does not become final until death.

Tony might consider allocating voting and non-voting company shares to all three children. This would provide his daughter with an equally valued distribution with potential for growth while still keeping voting control with his active sons. In addition, the implementation of a performance-based compensation plan would further reward his sons for their active role in the successful management of the business. If Tony decides to go this route, he should formalize this compensation plan today to avoid future conflict.

BUILDING SUPPORTIVE MANAGEMENT

Tony mentions that some of his senior managers are resisting retirement and having a hard time "letting go." Before he exits, Tony should act as the "third voice of reason" to address this problem. If the situation is left unresolved, the authority of his sons could be seriously undermined.

It is important for succeeding generations to build their own management teams with the levels of strength, experience and support that suit their particular needs. As a general rule, business transitions benefit when the new generation is able to select their own top people, whenever applicable.

9
FROM THE OUTSIDE LOOKING IN

In this chapter, we present the views of a non-family executive and his perspective of working in a family business.

Brian Tanner is a 55-year-old executive who has made a career out of working with family-controlled businesses. Typically, he has served as chief financial officer for companies with annual revenues in the range of $25 million to $120 million.

Working in this capacity has allowed Brian to put his knowledge of estate, tax and succession planning to good use. His broad range of experience also makes him well qualified to act as a mentor to family business owners.

Brian's specialty may be finance, but it is the human relations side of working for family-run businesses that he finds so rewarding.

With the exception of one brief stint with a large publicly traded corporation, I have spent my entire working career with family-controlled businesses. I have a master's degree in finance and a good working knowledge of estate, tax and succession planning. A family-run business gives me a lot of scope to use my skill sets. Apart from the number crunching, I also enjoy the opportunity to work as a mentor and educator. Family businesses need someone with experience to manage their risk and watch out for their interests.

Currently, Brian is working with two families that each own 50 percent of a large beverage-bottling company located in the Tampa Bay, Florida, area.

I started working for this company when the first-generation owners were preparing to exit. There are currently five brothers involved in the business but only four of them have an ownership position (when ownership was transferred from the first generation to the second, one of the family members was deemed not to have ownership). Ownership is not equally distributed since one individual owns 50 percent and the three brothers from the other family own the other 50 percent combined.

Three of the family members are actively involved in management in the capacities of chief executive officer, chief operating officer and vice president of sales.

I am about ten years older than the brothers. This was a consideration when they hired me since they made it clear they were looking for someone to serve as a mentor.

Brian's position as a non-family member gives him a different perspective on the company's operations.

I would say that from the standpoint of the employees, there is an element of confusion over who is in charge of this business. In my experience, this is often the case when more than one family is involved in the day-to-day operations of a firm, particularly when ownership is not equally distributed. There is also some confusion over the allocation of profits.

There are often times when I am put in the middle. In those situations, I make a point of remaining impartial. I remind myself that the goal of the business is to make money and I work for the company and the stockholders. As a consequence, I make decisions based on what is good for the company and not what is good for one particular family member or another.

Brian's neutral position is invaluable when it comes to assisting in the decision-making process.

When it comes to human resource issues such as employment policies, compensation and employee manuals, I provide the family members with the information they need, together with my personal recommendations. At that point, it is up to the family members to come to an agreement.

In my current position, I initiate quarterly meetings of the owners so we can have a good forum for open communication and the means to resolve conflict. Essentially, the owners talk the issue through until they reach consensus. All of the owners are intelligent, capable businessmen so it is not too difficult for good sense to prevail.

This is the first company I have worked for where two families each have 50 percent of the stock. In the event that agreement cannot be reached and there is a tied vote, it means trouble for the company. The secret of success for a small firm is being able to react to change quickly. This can only happen if management is able to make decisions fast. A stalemate situation can result in the loss of a good business opportunity.

While the owners have been quite successful at growing the business, this has tended to be at the expense of seeing the big picture. Brian is currently helping the owners put a succession plan in place.

The owners have been somewhat shortsighted about what they need to be doing today to maximize the value of the company down the road. In addition, they need to put safeguards in place to protect themselves in the event of divorce, death or incapacity. These are just some of the common factors that could adversely affect the business.

To assist in the succession planning process, we brought our bank in and determined what the company is worth on a cash flow basis. During this process, there was a lot of conflict over who was making what and how each owner was contributing to the overall picture. Personality differences can be quite a challenge at times! Each side of the family has its own advisor and is taking care of its own estate planning and insurance needs.

The biggest risk in not having a buy/sell agreement in place is what could happen on the death of the owner. If the spouse inherits the stock, then you run the risk of having their attorney telling you how to run your business. There is also the risk of someone selling his or her shares to a competitor. It's very important to have the company valued, be able to fund a buy out and have insurance in place. The older you are, the more expensive the insurance, but enough insurance should be in place to provide the capital for a buy out should the situation arise.

Much of what Brian does can best be described as education and support for the owners.

I have taken a company into – and out of – bankruptcy. I have been through the death of an owner with – and without – insurance. I have been in a situation in a publicly traded company where my superior was cooking the books because he figured that was the way to get a bonus.

Family business owners need to trust someone to manage their risk and look out for their interests. Often it's a steep learning curve. There have been times when the owners don't listen to me and have experienced problems. When that happens, I hope they will learn something for the next time and come to realize that, as a result of my objectivity and experience, I might know things they don't.

Brian would be the first to admit that his position is not always an easy one.

One of the essential requirements for someone working in my role is patience. I never expect to win a point the first time I present it. The best you can hope for is that, after a period of time, the owners will start listening. Right from your first day on the job, you have to work on gaining their trust. Sometimes you have to be the person who asks the hard questions and that's how you earn more respect.

However, as an employee you can only do so much. At the end of the day, you have to acknowledge that it's not your business and it's not your money. If the owners wish to make bad decisions, then, they have every right to do so. When I'm working for people who are making decisions based on emotion rather than reason, I try not to get angry or caught up in the family dynamics. I just try to do what's good for the company.

Despite the occasional frustrations, Brian enjoys the benefits that accrue from working for a relatively small family-owned business.

I personally find that working for a small business is much more interesting than working in the public arena. The smaller businesses allow a finance guy to move beyond the numbers and get involved in the operations side. Numbers in themselves can be a grind, but what job satisfaction really comes down to is the people. In my position, I get to work on the human side as well. Once you are in the think tank with a family business, you become indispensable. The third leg of every business is financial knowledge and acumen. If you are adept at providing banking advice, financial projections and tax planning, you can really add value to the company, for which you will be rewarded. The owners of this company certainly give back. We have a benefits program that rivals anything offered by a Fortune 500 company.

Of course, this isn't true of all family-owned businesses and, sometimes, blood is thicker than water. I have been known to leave a company if I felt I was not being adequately compensated, financially or personally, for the value I was adding. It isn't just the money; it's enjoying what I do.

Based on his years of experience in helping family-run businesses with their succession planning, Brian offers the following pointers for a smooth transition:

1) CREATING A PLAN

Owners should understand that they need a plan since, without strategic planning, they are doomed to failure. As the saying goes, "If you don't know where you're going, any road will take you there."

2) PREPARING FOR CHANGE

The only constant in life is change. When owners are caught up in the day-to-day concerns of running a business, it is easy to assume that things will stay just as they are. The reality is that one day the unthinkable will happen and you had better be prepared.

3) BUILDING STRONG MANAGEMENT

At some point in time, owners need to make themselves dispensable so their companies can succeed without them. By assembling a reliable management team – finance, sales and operations – owners can ensure their businesses can be effectively run with – or without – them.

4) BECOMING A PROFESSIONALLY RUN BUSINESS

Professionalizing a family-owned business is the key to protecting a family's assets. Most family-owned businesses never make the transition from privately held company to professionally run business. Instead, most owners take the "escape route" and sell the business regardless of whether this is the best course of action from the standpoint of asset preservation.

5) DEVELOPING TRUST

It is essential that an owner develop a management team that operates in a climate in which the key ingredient is trust.

Brian also highlights the two major impediments to successful succession planning he has experienced over the years:

1) LACK OF VISION

Many owners are guilty of focusing on the short run. They don't apply long-term vision to planning the big picture. Part of the problem is they tend to think they are going to live forever and fail to realize that change is the only thing on which you can count. A related problem is that many family businesses tend to shrink over time. They don't realize that they need to grow in order to survive.

2) LACK OF FINANCIAL PLANNING

Owners need to understand how finance works. They need to build strong relationships with their banks and understand that banks want to see a commitment to growth and capital accumulation. They should not strip the company of cash; it's important to keep the company off the edge. The bottom line is a bank is much less likely to invest in a company if there's no apparent long-term commitment from the owners.

FINAL THOUGHTS ON SUCCESSION PLANNING

When we decided to write a book about the critical importance of succession planning, we knew that the larger story would be best told through the words of our clients. Through the generosity of these clients, who have shared their thoughts and stories, we begin to see why so many families struggle with succession planning.

Emotions often override reason when a family faces the transition of a family business, and the so-called "soft issues" usually take precedence over technical challenges such as creating the most tax-effective strategy.

Certain issues are common to many family stories:

- Learning how to raise children to be stewards of wealth while at the same time, avoiding issues of entitlement and nepotism.

- Working with family members who have quite different visions for the future of the business – and different views on the effectiveness of management.

- Communicating effectively with the family in a manner that manages conflict.

- Addressing the conflict between an owner's dream of passing on the business to the next generation and the children's desire to fulfill their sometimes competing aspirations.

- Dealing with siblings who each have a sense of entitlement, yet who possess talents, skills and experience that may be inadequate.

- Handling family dynamics when children marry, have children of their own, separate or divorce.

- Facing and adapting to market changes and economic slowdowns.

The challenge of dealing with these difficult issues causes many family business owners to delay the establishment of a workable succession plan. However, this is an achievable goal for any family so long as the proper supports are in place.

To encourage families to take the first steps towards a successful business transition, Harris offers a manageable approach to the succession planning process. We help our clients work through the three essential steps that we believe are common to successful succession planning: goal setting, strategic planning, and implementation and exit.

While every client needs to work through these steps, our approach is tailored to the unique circumstances of your family business. At Harris, we begin by seeking a full understanding of your personal situation and only then suggest succession planning tools appropriate to your needs. After a thorough analysis, the planning process is broken down into manageable and measurable steps, and many options and resources are provided to assist you in the successful transfer of your business.

GOAL SETTING

This initial step forms the critical foundation for all that is to follow. We assist you in the process of determining your core values and goals. To do this, we ask your family to consider a number of questions: Are you committed to keeping the business in the family? Do you wish to sell the business? Do you wish to take a "wait-and-see" approach to keeping the business in the family?

Some of the questions are best answered if you have looked into the future as well as into your past. Your personal vision helps you to answer some fundamental questions such as where do you see the business in five years? Where do you see yourself in 10 years? What role does your family wish to play in the transition or sale of your business?

If your goal is to keep your business in the family, then we recommend turning the succession process into a family affair. Create an environment that fosters open communication and engages the next generation. Work together on plans, solutions and decision-making, ideally through family meetings using an objective facilitator who can help develop the essential skills for family communication. If part of the family's vision is to keep the business in the family, then the following are suggested courses of action for developing family governance with the help of your succession advisor:

- Craft a mission statement defining how the family wants to work together in the business.

- Establish a Family Council to provide a forum for family meetings. It is important to include family members and spouses of family members who are both active and inactive in the business. The Family Council will also provide a forum to educate and update family members on current challenges and plans for the business.

- Educate family members on ownership, stewardship and wealth-preservation issues.

- Resolve not only the question of ownership, but also the leadership and management of the company.

- Create family employment and development plans that outline appropriate compensation for family members working in the business.

STRATEGIC PLANNING

Once the goals are determined and the ground rules have been established, the next phase requires taking a step back and using your advisors to help determine how to meet your goals from both a business and family perspective.

Our focus at this stage is to work with the family to ensure continuity of the business during the transitioning process. We assist business owners in devising a methodology to analyze the business as an entity, separate from family and management concerns. A Strengths, Weaknesses, Opportunities and Threats (SWOT) analysis of your business is undertaken, which assesses the size and complexity of the business in addition to determining the business needs from an operating, financial and leadership point of view to ensure long-term viability.

Once the needs of the business – as distinct from family or shareholder concerns – are fully understood, the qualities required of a successor begin to emerge. If family transition is contemplated, then a succession development plan for a potential successor needs to be created. This will define the gaps that need to be filled in terms of both formal and informal education and detailing the experience that needs to be obtained from both inside and outside the business. Once in place, it is important that the successor development plan be monitored by a non-family mentor who is able to evaluate progress and establish a time line for meeting pre-determined goals.

IMPLEMENTATION AND EXIT

Once goals and a strategy are set, the family will have a clear direction about the future of the business, including whether it is to be kept in the family or sold to an outside party.

Typically, a succession plan consists of the family's mission for its business, the shareholders' agreement, the family participation plan, the business continuity plan, the successor development plan and the estate plan, including any philanthropic goals.

Ideally, the implementation of these plans leads to a well-managed and phased exit strategy for you, the business owner. Communicating with employees and customers regarding the succession plan is crucial. Employees will be grateful for the opportunity to be "in the know" at the appropriate time and will likely be more loyal to the business during the transition if they feel a part of the process. It is the air of uncertainty in some family business successions that has a demoralizing effect on employees. Customers and suppliers will also appreciate being advised of the proposed change in leadership.

Given the complex issues and emotional upheaval that often characterize a family transition, it is not surprising that many families opt to sell instead. However, planning the sale requires a great deal of attention and work, which can be a distraction from day-to-day operations.

Should the decision be made to sell the business, you will need to work with advisors on determining the value of the business in addition to creating a desired timeline for the sale of and exit from the business.

Apart from maximizing after-tax sale proceeds, other considerations, such as confidentiality, timing and ease of execution, are common issues that affect the way a family chooses to market and sell their family business.

There are families that attempt to sell their businesses without the help of their advisors or an intermediary. This do-it-yourself approach can have a negative effect on the value of the business and the stability of key employees, and is, therefore, generally not advisable. Emotions experienced during the negotiation process often cloud good business judgment. It is always better to take advantage of the objectivity of experienced professionals.

Regardless of whether the business is sold or transferred within the family, owners are encouraged to set aside some time for retirement and estate planning. Without a plan in place, many owners find the challenge of no longer being actively involved in the business difficult to bear. In these cases, a great deal of confusion and conflict can occur between the departed owner and the succeeding generation. For this reason, retiring owners are strongly encouraged to engage in a phased-exit plan, after which they may look forward to achieving their personal retirement goals, including travel and possibly philanthropic initiatives.

In this final phase of implementing the succession plan, a key consideration is the financial security of the exiting business owner. A family business that can afford to cash out the owner has a huge advantage over the situation where the departing owner is dependent on the continued profitability of the business and liquidity is frequently an issue. However, creative planning can find ways around this problem. Succession plans should be reviewed and updated on an ongoing basis to ensure they adequately reflect changes in the family and business dynamics. While effective succession planning is challenging, the good news is that we know from experience that a positive outcome is possible. The hard part is getting started, but with guidance from knowledgeable professionals and experienced advisors, you will clearly be up to the challenge.